VOICES IN LITERATURE

Mary Lou McCloskey • Lydia Stack

Heinle & Heinle Publishers • A Division of Wadsworth, Inc. • Boston, Massachusetts 02116 U.S.A.

The publication of *Voices in Literature Silver* was directed by the members of the Heinle & Heinle Secondary ESL Publishing Team:

Editorial Director: Roseanne Mendoza
Senior Production Services Coordinator: Lisa McLaughlin
Market Development Director: Ingrid Greenberg

Also participating in the publication of this program were:

Vice President and Publisher: Stanley J. Galek
Director of Production: Elizabeth Holthaus
Senior Assistant Editor: Sally Conover
Manufacturing Coordinator: Mary Beth Hennebury
Project Management/Composition/Design: Ligature, Inc.

Cover art: Henri Matisse, "The Snail"

ISBN: 0-8384-7019-X
Manufactured in the United States of America.

Heinle & Heinle
An International Thomson Publishing Company
Boston, Massachusetts 02116 U.S.A.

10   9   8   7   6   5   4

Dedicated to D. Scott Enright for his inspiration, enthusiasm, and support, which sustained us from initial idea through writer's block to creative frenzy as *Voices in Literature* came to be.

The authors and publisher would like to acknowledge the contributions of the following individuals who reviewed or field-tested *Voices in Literature* at various stages of development and who offered many helpful insights and suggestions.

Consultants

Nina Glaudini Rosen
Glendale (CA) Community College

Keith Buchanan
Fairfax County (VA) Public Schools

Linda Sasser
Alhambra (CA) School District

Reviewers

Stephen Sloan
Los Angeles Unified School District

Carol Anastasi
Boston Public Schools

Alfredo Schifini
California State University, Los Angeles

Flo Decker
El Paso (TX) Independent School District

Dorothy Taylor
Buffalo (NY) School District

Mary Wayne Pierce
Hartford Public Schools

Anne Elmkies
Hartford Public Schools

Joyce Smith
Northeast ISD, San Antonio (TX)

Leslie Jean Rolph
San Diego High School

Judy Schilling
Gwinnett County (GA) Public Schools

Patsy Thompson
Gwinnett County (GA) Public Schools

Jackie Macabasco
San Francisco Unified School District

Christina Pehl
San Francisco Unified School District

Kate Bamberg
San Francisco Unified School District

Acknowledgments

The authors would like to thank our husbands, Joel Reed and Jim Stack, as well as our children, Tom, Sean, Kevin, Dierdre, and Erin for their support and understanding during our sometimes lengthy coast-to-coast trips and conversations.

We thank Meg Morris, Erik Gundersen, and John Chapman for their support through the editorial process of producing this book, Anne Spencer and Ligature, Inc. for helping us make it so beautiful, and Laura Runge, Nathalie Kinkade, and Jodi Cressman for invaluable help in creating the manuscript.

Finally, we gratefully acknowledge Chris Foley and Heinle & Heinle Publishers for listening to secondary ESOL teachers and responding with a quality book which is innovative and timely.

(continued on p. 210)

Welcome to *Voices in Literature*. This book was written so that you, students from many cultures and language backgrounds, could learn English, learn to talk about literature, and explore themes that are found in many cultures. We have tried to find selections that will help you learn about North American culture, selections about moving from one culture to another, and selections that reflect the many cultures that make up North America. We hope that some of the selections will remind you of experiences and stories of your families and friends.

Many of the activities in the book are meant to be done in pairs or small groups. You will work with other students to solve problems and design projects that reflect not only your own thinking but also new ideas you and your classmates will discover by working in groups. In most cases, there is no one right answer or one way to do an activity. You will have choices to make, and the products will reflect your creativity and hard work.

You will need to expand the English you use so that you can talk about the literature, find out what it means to you, and make others understand your point of view. You will learn new language from the authors, your teachers, and your fellow students.

In the first unit, *Beginnings*, you will explore literature that uses the sun as a symbol of a new beginning. The second unit, *Origins*, examines creation stories from many cultures. Unit Three is about *Friendship* and how friends help and support one another. In Unit Four, you will look at *Wishes and Dreams* in both real and imaginary situations. In Unit Five, you will discover how *Generations* (family members from different age groups) work, play, and learn together.

We hope you enjoy *Voices in Literature*. We would love to hear your ideas and opinions about it.

Mary Lou McCloskey
Lydia Stack

Voices in Literature provides teachers and students of English for speakers of other languages (ESOL) an anthology of high quality literature. The selections and the activities for using those selections will help students interact with literature to benefit their language learning, to foster literary discussion, and to introduce to students the language and concepts of literature. A variety of ways for teachers and students to approach the literature selections, to interact with the actual texts, and to respond to the selections have been included.

Why use literature?

Literature is an appropriate, valuable, and valid medium to assist ESOL students in accomplishing important goals. Literature provides students with motivation to learn and models of high quality language while it enhances students' imagination, interaction, and collaboration.

Motivation. Literature motivates students by touching on themes they care about, such as love, fear, changes, and dreams. Good literature is about the human experience; it is meaningful to students from different linguistic and cultural backgrounds.

Models. Carefully chosen literature provides models of high quality language with sophistication and complexity appropriate to students' age level. Literature offers new vocabulary in context and serves as a source for learning about the mechanics of language in authentic contexts, as they are used by masters of that language.

Imagination. Imagination is one of the abilities that makes us fully human. Literature can give students the means to imagine and think creatively. Literature demands that the reader step into the author's world; good literature demands thought from the reader. Students who are learning a new language need and deserve the challenges to their imaginations which appropriate literature provides.

Interaction and collaboration. Language is learned best in a setting in which it is put to use. Literature provides a common text from which students can negotiate meaning. Well-selected literature addresses issues that are vital to young readers and that stimulate lively discussion among students. Using literature in combination with collaborative activities helps students to understand the literature better, to relate it to their own ideas and experiences and to go beyond the literature to produce their own literature-related products.

What kinds of literature should be used?

In selecting texts for *Voices in Literature*, we have used a broad definition of literature and have included fiction, nonfiction, poetry, songs, drama, and speeches. We sought authentic and rich texts that provide real, high quality language models. We feel that there is no need to "water down" the literature we use with ESOL students; we just need to choose it carefully. In making selections, we were also guided by the following concerns:

Student interest. Literature should be age-appropriate and should address themes of interest to the learners.

Linguistic accessibility. The language of the literature should be clear and simple enough for the student to understand, yet it must be expressive, figurative, and evocative to match the maturity and intellectual sophistication of the students. We have included, for example, many poetry selections. Poetry is simple—often using rhyme, rhythm, and repetition to enhance comprehensibility—yet also complex, evoking deep emotion and thoughts in the reader.

Cultural relevance. Literature selected for ESOL students should reflect many cultures, address concerns of individuals who are experiencing cultural change, and teach about the new, English-speaking culture.

How can literature be used effectively in the ESOL classroom?

We have used a variety of strategies and structures to support students as they learn language through literature and study literature through language. Thematic organization offers students opportunities to relate concepts and works of literature to one another. The revisitation of themes, ideas, and terms provides enhanced context and thus improves comprehensibility. The supportive format we offer follows an "into-through-beyond" model that includes activities for use before, during, and after reading the literature.

Before you read. We use connections to students' own experience as well as background information about the literature to guide them "into" the work.

The selection. We provide a variety of ways to guide students "through" the work.

After you read. Finally, we use thought-provoking discussion questions, cooperative learning activities, experiences to expand comprehension of literary concepts and terms, writing activities, project ideas, and suggested further readings to take students "beyond" the work into their own high-level thinking and original creations. At the end of each unit, we include activities to help students relate the works to one another around the unit themes.

We hope that you and your students enjoy using the selections and activities in *Voices in Literature* and that they enrich your classroom learning community. We would love to hear from you about your experiences with our book.

Mary Lou McCloskey
Lydia Stack

Table of Contents

Unit 2   Origins

Unit 3 Friendship

Good Afternoon II by Alex Katz

2

U N I T

1

Beginnings

*The first part of this
book is about beginnings.
You will read poems
about the beginning of
a new day and about
starting a new part of
your life. You'll hear a
song about the sun rising
and read a story about
the first day of school.*

▶ *Exploring Your Own Experience*

Before you read the poem, think and talk about how you, your teacher, and your classmates begin the morning.

Think-Pair-Share

1. First, think for a few minutes about the way you start the day. How do you feel when you wake up? Sleepy? Wide awake? What do you do when you first get up in the morning? What do other people in your family do? Do you wake up to the radio? Do you get up early? Late? Do you eat a big breakfast? Do you dress before breakfast?
2. Next, tell a partner what you are thinking.
3. Finally, with your partner, sit with another pair of students. Take turns talking, each person telling what his or her partner said.

Making a Chart

When you finish your discussion, your class or group might make a chart to show how people in the class begin the day. Below is a sample chart that one class made. What can you say about your class based on your chart? Do most people get up early? Do they eat a big breakfast?

▶ *Background*

This poem was written by an American author who lives in the desert in Arizona. She writes about how people from many times and places greet the sun at the beginning of the day.

The poem has different parts. Each part is about how to greet the new day.

Wake up to radio	Wake up to sun	Get up early	Sleep late	Eat a big breakfast	Eat a small breakfast
Ngo	Tom	Judy	Jorge	Judy	Hyung
Jorge	Esther	Hyung	Angie	Tom	Ngo
			Ngo		Esther

The Way to Start a Day

by
Byrd Baylor

The way to start a day
is this—

Go outside
and face the east
and greet the sun
with some kind of
blessing
or chant
or song
that you made yourself
and keep for
early morning.

The way to make the song
is this—

Don't try to think
what words to use

....

greet to meet, welcome
blessing prayer of good wishes
chant rhythmic, repeated group
of words

Desert Ridges Sunrise, San Pedro River Valley, Arizona by David Muench.

until
you're standing there
alone.

When you feel the sun
you'll feel
the song too.

Just sing it.

But
don't think you're
the only one
who ever worked
that magic.

Your caveman brothers
knew what to do.
Your cavewoman sisters
knew too.
They sang
to help the sun
come up
and lifted their hands
to its power.

....

magic unexplained power
caveman, cavewoman people
who lived in caves before written
history
power strength

A morning
needs
to be sung to.
A new day
needs
to be honored.

People
have always
known that.

Didn't they chant
at dawn
in the sun temples
of Peru?

And leap and sway
to Aztec flutes
in Mexico?

And drum
sunrise songs
in the Congo?

....

honored respected
chant sing or say with repeated
rhythm and words
temples places to worship God
leap jump
sway move from side to side
Congo country in central Africa,
now called Zaire

And ring
a thousand
small gold bells
in China?

Didn't the pharaohs
of Egypt
say
the only
sound
at dawn
should be
the sound of
songs
that please
the morning sun?

They knew
what songs
to sing.

People
always
seemed to know.

And
everywhere
they knew

....

pharaohs rulers in Egypt long ago

what gifts
the sun
wanted.

In some places
they gave
gold.
In some places
they gave
flowers.
In some places,
sacred smoke
blown to the four
directions.
Some places,
feathers
and good thoughts.
Some places,
fire.

But
everywhere
they knew
to give
something.

....

sacred holy
eastward toward the east

Ashanti Gold soul washers' badge

And
everywhere
they knew
to turn
their faces
eastward
as the sun
came up.

Some people
still
know.

When the first
pale
streak of light
cuts
through the
darkness,
wherever they are,
those people
make offerings

....

pale softly colored
streak long, thin strip
through in one side and out the
other side of
make offerings give things
mysterious unexplained

and send
strong
mysterious
songs
to the sun.

They know
exactly
how to start
a day.

....

mysterious unexplained,
strange

ABOUT THE AUTHOR

Byrd Baylor, born in 1924, grew up in the deserts of the southwestern United States. She tells about her love for nature and this area in many of her books. Her works show her sense of wonder, her respect for nature, and her interest in the past.

▶ **Byrd Baylor (born 1924)** ◀

AFTER YOU READ

▶ *What Do You Think?*

Think about the poem and discuss your ideas with your classmates and teacher. Here are some other ideas and questions to talk about:

1. What ways does the author give for greeting the day? How does the author tell you how you will know what to say when greeting the day?
2. How have people from other times and places "worked that magic" of greeting the day? What did the cavemen and cavewomen do to greet the sun?
3. What gifts were offered to the sun?
4. Why do people greet the sun? What is their hope for a new day?
5. How do people in your culture greet the sun? Is it like any of the ways in this poem?
6. How does the author, Byrd Baylor, describe people greeting the sun in different cultures? What makes these descriptions so clear?

▶ *Try This* AM

Charting the Poem

Make a chart like the one below listing all the places in the poem. Then fill in as much as you can. A globe and maps can help you.

People	Country	Continent	What they did to greet the sun	What they do now
Cave People	Countries	Asia	Sang	These people
	didn't exist	Europe		are now gone
	then.	Africa		
People in the	Peru			
Sun temples				

▶ Learning About Literature

How are Poems Different from Other Kinds of Writing?

1. There are many kinds of poems. Poems can tell stories or describe feelings or things that happen. They can be silly or serious. How are poems different from other kinds of writing? One way is how they look on the page. Compare p. 5 (a poem) with p. 29 (prose). How do the pages look different?

2. *Prose* is speech or writing that does not have rhyme or meter and is not poetry. Prose writers usually use paragraphs to separate their thoughts. Poets don't have to use paragraphs. They can arrange the words in many ways to tell what they mean.

   In "The Way to Start a Day," the poet uses *stanzas*. A stanza is a group of lines. Extra space is left between stanzas. Stanzas can separate different ideas in a poem, and they can help you know when to *pause*, or wait for a second, when reading the poem out loud. What is the shortest stanza in the poem? The longest? Find a stanza in the poem that you like and read it to a partner.

3. Choose a favorite stanza. Record it on tape or recite it before the class. You may choose to memorize the stanza.

▶ Writing

Getting Ready to Write

The charts you made before and after reading "The Way to Start a Day" can help you get ready to write. They are a way to collect and organize your ideas.

1. **Write about a chart.** Use either the chart you made before reading or the one you made after reading to help you write about ways that people start the day. Don't try to write about all of the ways: use only a few.

2. **Write your own stanza.** Continue "The Way to Start a Day" with your ideas about the best way to start a day. Write your own greeting to the sun. Why are you glad to see the sun again? What is your hope for the new day?

3. **Write your own poem.** Choose a topic you care about and write a poem. You may want to compare different ways of doing something. Or, you may have your own idea. Use a chart to get ready to write.

▶ *Exploring Your Own Experience* AM

Have you ever watched the sun rise? Where were you? Why were you there? Whom were you with? What did you think about? How did you feel? One way to organize your answers to these questions is on a "sunshine outline" like the one below. After completing the outline, discuss it with your classmates.

▶ *Background*

This is a song written by George Harrison, a member of the Beatles, a world-famous singing group from the 1960s. "Here Comes the Sun" is from the Beatles' *Abbey Road* album.

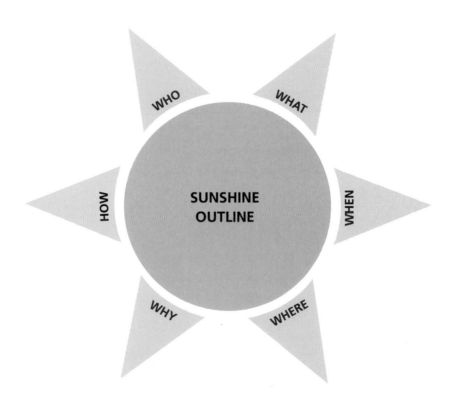

WHO WHAT HOW **SUNSHINE OUTLINE** WHEN WHY WHERE

Here Comes the Sun

by

George Harrison

Here comes the sun, here comes the sun,
And I say it's all right.
Little darling it's been a long cold lonely winter
Little darling it feels like years since it's been here.

Here comes the sun, here comes the sun,
And I say it's all right.

Little darling the smiles returning to their faces,
Little darling it seems like years since it's been here,

Here comes the sun, here comes the sun,
And I say it's all right.

---

darling dear person, sweetheart
lonely feeling alone

Red Hills and Sun, Lake George by Georgia O'Keeffe, 1956.

Sun, sun, sun, here it comes.
Sun, sun, sun, here it comes.
Sun, sun, sun, here it comes.
Sun, sun, sun, here it comes.

Little darling I feel that ice is slowly melting,
Little darling it seems like years since it's been clear,

Here comes the sun, here comes the sun,
It's all right, it's all right.

---

melting turning from ice into water

ABOUT THE SONGWRITER

George Harrison, one of the world's top rock-'n'-roll musicians, grew up in a working-class area of Liverpool, England. He became interested in rock-'n'-roll when he was twelve, and he bought a used guitar at thirteen. By seventeen he was playing music with John Lennon and Paul McCartney in a group called the Quarrymen. This group later became the Beatles. The popular song, "Here Comes the Sun," tells how people were feeling in the late 1960s.

 George Harrison (born 1943) ◀

▶ *What Do You Think?*

Think about the song and discuss your ideas with your classmates and your teacher. Then think and talk about some of the ideas below.

1. What do you think the sun stands for in this song?
2. "Smiles are returning to the faces" seems to say that something good is starting to happen. What other words tell you that something good is coming? What are all the signs that there will be a change for the better?
3. Some people think that George Harrison was talking about the whole world when he wrote this song. The words "the ice is slowly melting" might mean that some countries are beginning to become friendlier with each other. Think about what some of the other words in the song might mean about our world. Make a list to share with the class.

▶ *Try This*

Walking Gallery

Here is a chance to find out what your classmates think about the song.

1. Get into groups of about four.
2. Each group should draw a picture of what they imagine when they listen to the song "Here Comes the Sun."
   Important: Each person must draw some part of the picture.
3. When your pictures are finished, take your picture to another group. Tell that group about your picture.
   Important: Each person in the group should tell something about the picture.
4. Listen to what people in that group tell you about their picture. What new ideas did you hear about?

▶ Learning About Literature

Symbol

1. A symbol is something that stands for something else. Some symbols are pictures. A flag can be a symbol for a country. The sun is a popular symbol for happiness or for a new beginning. What do the symbols below mean to you?

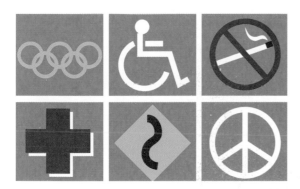

2. Sometimes words are used as symbols. For example, the word "winter" can mean a period of difficulties or sadness. What other words in "Here Comes the Sun" are used as symbols? What do you think they mean?
3. Look for symbols in newspapers, magazines, and books. Look for pictures that are symbols as well as words that are symbols. Make a bulletin-board display of the symbols you find.

▶ Writing

Getting Ready to Write

Sunshine outlines like the one shown before "Here Comes the Sun" can be used to get ready to write. After choosing your topic, use a sunshine outline to help you list what you want to write about. Answer the questions, who?, what?, when?, where?, why?, and how? about your topic.

1. Choose a symbol from the book or bulletin board. Write about what it might stand for.
2. Make up a story that tells more about the changes happening in "Here Comes the Sun."
3. Write about a change in your life. Can you think of a symbol for that change to use in your story or in the title?

▶ Exploring Your Own Experience AM

What's Behind the Door?

You will be reading a poem about going through doors. It might make you think about the new and unknown things that are behind the doors of your future life.

Before you read the poem "Prospective Immigrant, Please Note," use this activity to share some ideas about what the future holds for you.

1. Take out two sheets of paper. Fold one into quarters. Label the quarters, "Education," "Career," "Family," and "Achievements."

2. In each box, draw a picture of yourself in the future. For example, in the "Education" box, draw a picture of you in a school you will attend in the future.

3. Fold the second sheet of paper into quarters and cut out "doors" that open from each. Put this over your first paper. Label the doors with the same labels.

4. Work with a partner to guess what is behind each other's doors. Open the doors to show if the guesses were right or wrong.

▶ Background

The first time you read the poem you will not understand everything. Read it several more times and see which parts become clearer. Use the footnotes to help you understand new words. Make guesses about what each stanza means, even if you aren't sure.

The words of a poem will mean different things to different people. Poems can be understood in many ways. After reading this poem, you will compare your understanding of it with what others think. You may be surprised at how many different ways people see this poem.

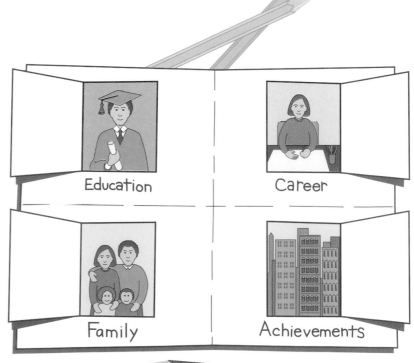

"Prospective Immigrants, Please Note"

by
Adrienne Rich

Either you will
go through this door
or you will not go through.

If you go through
there is always the risk
of remembering your name.

Things look at you doubly
and you must look back
and let them happen

If you do not go through
it is possible
to live worthily

....

risk chance
doubly two times; two ways
worthily in a good way

Rooms by the Sea by Edward Hopper

to maintain your attitudes
to hold your position
to die bravely

but much will blind you,
much will evade you,
at what cost who knows?

The door itself
makes no promises.
It is only a door.

....

attitudes ways of acting or feeling
hold your position stay where you are
bravely not afraid
blind to make unable to see
evade escape, get away from

ABOUT THE AUTHOR

Adrienne Rich was born in Baltimore, Maryland, in 1929. She was educated at home by her parents, a doctor and a musician, until the fourth grade. Her early poems used controlled form. Her later poems are more revolutionary, exploring hopes and experiences of women.

▶ **Adrienne Rich (born 1929)** ◀

▶ *What Do You Think?*

Think about the poem and discuss your ideas with your classmates and teacher. Here are some other ideas to talk about.

1. Remember that a symbol stands for something else. What does the door stand for in this poem?
2. Do you understand all of the words? If not, ask your teacher and classmates to help you.
3. How many stanzas are in the poem? How long is each stanza? Can you put into your own words what each stanza is saying?
4. Who is the immigrant in the poem? What is that person choosing? Read the lines that helped you find these answers.
5. What do you think will happen if the person goes through the door? What will happen if he/she doesn't go through?
6. What does the poet mean by "there is always the risk / of remembering your name"?

▶ *Try This*

Round Table

In groups of about four, try working with some new symbols.

1. One person writes a word or draws a picture at the top of a sheet of paper.
2. The following person writes or draws pictures that the previous words or pictures remind him or her of.
3. Pass the paper around the circle several times. You can help each other at any time.
4. A person from each group can show the list and pictures to the class. Discuss what you learned from the activity.

▶ Learning About Literature

Tone

People often talk about the *tone* of a poem. They mean the feeling or mood it gives to the readers. Some poems may make you feel happy or carefree. Others are sad or serious.

1. What is the tone of this poem? How does it compare with the tone of "The Way to Start a Day" or "Here Comes the Sun"?

2. What kind of weather does this poem remind you of? What lines give you that feeling? Read them aloud to the class. Try to show your feelings with your voice.

▶ Writing

Using a Picture to Get Started

Drawing can help you get ready to write. Look at the two writing ideas below. Try drawing a picture of what you choose to write about. Label all of the parts of the picture. Use an English dictionary or translation dictionary to help you with the labels. Try using some of these new words in your writing.

1. Write about a "door" that you have gone through in your life. How did your life change? How did the way you think about yourself change?

2. Write about a "door" that you hope to pass through in your life. How will it change you? What dangers will you face in passing through the door?

▶ *Exploring Your Own Experience*

Brainstorming

Think about your first day in a new school. What are some words that tell how you felt? Someone can list on the chalkboard all the words you and your classmates can think of. This activity is called "brainstorming" or "word shaking" and is used to gather many ideas in a short time.

Two-Column Chart

Look at the chart below. Someone has started to fill it in. The left column lists things that made the first day at a new school easier. The right column shows things that made it harder.

Following this example, make your own chart of things that make your first day at a new school better or worse. You can use the list on the chalkboard to think of ideas. Do this activity alone, or write your ideas on the chalkboard.

▶ *Background*

Bette Bao Lord wrote a book about a girl who moved from China to Brooklyn, New York. It is based on the real life of the author. The following chapter describes the girl's first day in a new school.

The chapter is divided into five sections. You may want to stop at the end of each section to talk about the story with your classmates or teacher.

Things that made my first day at a new school easier	Things that made my first day at a new school harder
1. Someone gave me a pencil.	1. I couldn't find the rooms.
2. The principal smiled at me.	2. The teacher talked too fast.

China's Little Ambassador

from

In the Year of the Boar and Jackie Robinson,
by Bette Bao Lord

NINE O'CLOCK THE VERY NEXT morning, Shirley sat in the principal's office at P.S. 8. Her mother and the schoolmistress were talking. Shirley didn't understand a word. It was embarrassing. Why hadn't she, too, studied the English course on the records that Father had sent? But it was too late now. She stopped trying to understand. Suddenly, Mother hissed, in Chinese, "Stop that or else!"

Shirley snapped her head down. She had been staring at the stranger. But she could not keep her eyes from rolling up again. There was something more foreign about the principal than about any other foreigner she had seen so far. What was it? It was not the blue eyes. Many others had them too. It was not the high nose. All foreign noses were higher than Chinese ones. It was not the blue hair. Hair came in all colors in America.

Yes, of course, naturally. The woman had no eyelashes. Other foreigners grew hair all over them, more than six Chinese together. This woman had none. Her skin was as bare as the Happy Buddha's belly, except for the neat rows of stiff curls that hugged her head.

She had no eyebrows, even. They

P.S. 8 Public School 8

schoolmistress principal

embarrassing causing one to feel unhappy, self-conscious, or uncomfortable

records phonograph albums or recordings of music or instruction

foreign from another country

foreigner someone from another country

eyelashes tiny hairs on an eyelid

eyebrows hairs directly above the eyes

were penciled on, and looked just like the character for man, 人. And every time she tilted her head, her hair moved all in one piece like a hat.

"Shirley."

Mother was trying to get her attention. "Tell the principal how old you are."

Shirley held up ten fingers.

While the principal filled out a form, mother argued excitedly. But why? Shirley had given the correct answer. She counted just to make sure. On the day she was born, she was one year old. And two months later, upon the new year, she was two. That was the Year of the Rabbit. Then came the Dragon, Snake, Horse, Sheep, Monkey, Rooster, Dog and now it was the year of the Boar, making ten. Proof she was ten.

Mother shook her head. Apparently, she had lost her argument. She announced in Chinese, "Shirley, you will enter fifth grade."

"Fifth? But, Mother, I don't speak English. And besides, I only completed three grades in Chungking."

"I know. But the principal has explained that in America everyone is assigned according to age. Ten years old means fifth grade. And we must observe the American rules, mustn't we?"

Shirley nodded obediently. But she could not help thinking that only Shirley had to go to school, and only Shirley would be in trouble if she failed.

Mother stood up to leave. She took Shirley by the hand. "Remember, my daughter, you may be the only Chinese these Americans will ever meet. Do your best. Be extra good. Upon your shoulders rests the reputation of all Chinese."

All five hundred million? Shirley wondered.

"You are China's little ambassador."

"Yes, Mother." Shirley squared her shoulders and tried to feel worthy of this great honor. At the same time she wished she could leave with Mother.

Alone, the schoolmistress and Shirley looked at each other. Suddenly

---

get her attention make Shirley look at or listen to
proof test of the truth; facts that show the truth
apparently in a way easy to see

according to by
observe follow, act by
obediently following the rules
reputation way people think about you
ambassador an important person sent by one country to another

the principal shut one eye, the right one, then opened it again.

Was this another foreign custom, like shaking hands? It must be proper if a principal does it, Shirley thought. She ought to return the gesture, but she didn't know how. So she shut and opened both eyes. Twice.

This brought a warm laugh.

THE PRINCIPAL THEN LED HER TO class. The room was large, with windows up to the ceiling. Row after row of students, each one unlike the next. Some faces were white, like clean plates; others black like ebony. Some were in-between shades. A few were spotted all over. One boy was as big around as a water jar. Several others were as thin as chopsticks. No one wore a uniform of blue, like hers. There were sweaters with animals on them, shirts with stripes and shirts with squares, dresses in colors as varied as Grand-grand Uncle's paints. Three girls even wore earrings.

While Shirley looked about, the principal had been making a speech.

Suddenly it ended with "Shirley Temple Wong." The class stood up and waved.

Amitabha! They were all so tall. Even Water Jar was a head taller than she. For a fleeting moment she wondered if Mother would consider buying an ambassador a pair of high-heeled shoes.

"Hi, Shirley!" The class shouted.

Shirley bowed deeply. Then, taking a guess, she replied, "Hi!"

The teacher introduced herself and showed the new pupil to a front-row seat. Shirley liked her right away, although she had a most difficult name, Mrs. Rappaport. She was a tiny woman with dainty bones and fiery red hair brushed skyward. Shirley thought that in her previous life she must have been a bird, a cardinal perhaps. Yet she commanded respect, for no student talked out of turn. Or was it the long mean pole that hung on the wall behind the desk that commanded respect? It dwarfed the bamboo cane the teacher in Chungking had used to punish Four Hands whenever he stole

---

custom way of acting

gesture movement

ebony hard, black wood

chopsticks two small sticks used for eating in some Asian countries

uniform special clothes for school or work

dainty small

fiery like fire

previous earlier, one before

commanded respect made people do what she wanted

dwarfed was taller than

School's Out by Allen R. Crite

a trifle from another.

Throughout the lessons, Shirley leaned forward, barely touching her seat, to catch the meaning, but the words sounded like gurgling water. Now and then, when Mrs. Rappaport looked her way, she opened and shut her eyes as the principal had done, to show friendship.

AT LUNCHTIME, SHIRLEY WENT with the class to the school cafeteria, but before she could pick up a tray, several boys and girls waved for her to follow them. They were smiling, so she went along. They snuck back to the classroom to pick up coats, then hurried out the door and across the school yard to a nearby store. Shirley was certain they should not be there, but what choice did she have? These were now her friends.

One by one they gave their lunch money to the store owner, whom they called "Mr. P." In return, he gave each a bottle of orange-colored water, bread twice the size of an ear of corn oozing with meat balls, peppers, onions, and hot red gravy, and a large piece of brown paper to lay on the icy sidewalk and sit upon. While they ate, everyone except Shirley played marbles or cards and traded bottle caps and pictures of men swinging a stick or wearing one huge glove. It was the best lunch Shirley had ever had.

And there was more. After lunch, each of them was allowed to select one item from those displayed under the glass counter. There were paper strips dotted with red and yellow sugar tacks, chocolate soldiers in blue tin foil, boxes of raisins and nuts, envelopes of chips, cookies as big as pancakes, candy elephants, lollipops in every color, a wax collection of red lips, white teeth, pink ears and curly black mustaches. Shirley was the last to make up her mind. She chose a hand, filled with juice. It looked better than it tasted, but she did not mind. Tomorrow she could choose again.

---

trifle a small or unimportant thing or item
gurgling water water making noise as it goes over rocks
snuck went very quietly so no one would see
marbles a game with small glass balls

tacks small, round candies that come on strips of paper
tin foil aluminum foil or wrap
chips potato chips or corn chips
make up her mind decide

BUT WHEN SHE WAS BACK IN HER seat, waiting for Mrs. Rappaport to enter the classroom, Shirley's knees shook. What if the teacher found out about her escapade? There would go her ambassadorship. She would be shamed. Her parents would lose face. All five hundred million Chinese would suffer. Round and round in her stomach the meat balls tumbled like pebbles.

Then Mrs. Rappaport came in. She did not look pleased. Shirley flinched when the teacher went straight to the long mean pole. For the first time her heart went out to Four Hands. She shut her eyes and prayed to the Goddess of Mercy. Oh Kwan Yin, please don't let me cry! She waited, listening for Mrs. Rappaport's footsteps to become louder and louder. They did not. Finally curiosity overcame fear and she looked up. Mrs. Rappaport was using the pole to open a window!

The lessons continued. During arithmetic, Shirley raised her hand.

She went to the blackboard and wrote the correct answer. Mrs. Rappaport rewarded her with a big smile. Shirley opened and shut her eyes to show her pleasure.

Soon, she was dreaming about candy elephants and cookies the size of pancakes.

Then school was over. As Shirley was putting on her coat, Mrs. Rappaport handed her a letter, obviously to be given to her parents. Fear returned. Round and round, this time like rocks.

SHE BARELY GREETED HER MOTHER at the door.

"What happened?"

"Nothing."

"You look sick."

"I'm all right."

"Perhaps it was something you ate at lunch?"

"No," she said much too quickly. "Nothing at all to do with lunch."

"What then?"

---

escapade wild adventure

shamed lose respect, feel small

lose face lose respect, feel small

tumbled tossed and churned

flinched jumped back

curiosity need to know

rewarded gave a nice surprise to

obviously in a way easy to see

"The job of ambassador is harder than I thought."

At bedtime, Shirley could no longer put off giving up the letter. Trembling, she handed it to Father. She imagined herself on a boat back to China.

He read it aloud to Mother. Then they both turned to her, a most quizzical look on their faces.

"Your teacher suggests that we take you to a doctor. She thinks there is something wrong with your eyes."

---

trembling shaking

imagined pictured in her mind
quizzical questioning

ABOUT THE AUTHOR

Bette Bao Lord was born in Shanghai, China, in 1938. Her book *In the Year of the Boar and Jackie Robinson* tells of her experience moving from Shanghai to Brooklyn, New York, when she was eight years old. Her mother's dream was that she would grow up to be an "ist"—a chemist, physicist, or other scientist. She failed at chemistry, but did, at last, become an "ist"—a novelist. Her first book was *Eighth Moon*, the true story of her sister who grew up in China and was separated from her family for sixteen years.

 Bette Bao Lord (born 1938) ◄

▶ *What Do You Think?*

Think about the story and discuss your ideas with your classmates and teacher. Then think and talk about the ideas below. There are questions about each part of the story. Sometimes you will need to go back to the story to explain your ideas.

Pages 29-31

1. Did the story begin in a way that made you want to keep reading? Why or why not? Read aloud sentences that show why you think the way you do.

2. Who are the important characters? Describe each one briefly. What details does the author use to help you understand what each person is like?

3. What does Shirley's mother mean when she tells Shirley, "You are China's little ambassador"?

Pages 31-33

4. How does Shirley describe her classmates? What are some of the comparisons she uses? Which ones seem funny to you?

5. What does Shirley think of the classroom? What is she surprised about? What is she afraid of?

6. What does Shirley's teacher look like? How does Shirley feel about her?

Pages 33-34

7. Where does Shirley go at lunchtime? Does she enjoy herself? How do you know?

Pages 34-35

8. How does Shirley feel when she returns from lunch? What is she afraid of?

9. What does Mrs. Rappaport give Shirley at the end of the day? How does this make Shirley feel?

Page 35

10. What does the note from the teacher say? What did you think it was going to say?

11. Why did the teacher think something was wrong with Shirley's eyes?

12. Is there anything you did in your country that is misunderstood in the United States?

13. Can you make any comparisons between Shirley Temple Wong and the immigrant in Adrienne Rich's poem?

▶ *Try This* AM

What Is Your Point of View?

There is an old saying, "There are two sides to every story." This means that each person in a situation sees it a little differently from the others. Each one has his or her own "point of view," or understanding of the situation.

You can look at the story "China's Little Ambassador" from the point of view of Shirley, her mother, the schoolmistress, Mrs. Rappaport, or Shirley's classmates.

Try this role-playing activity. Each group chooses one character and uses a sunshine outline to make up questions to ask the person in the story. Use the sample outline to get started. Then one person from each group will pretend to be someone from the story. That person will answer the questions.

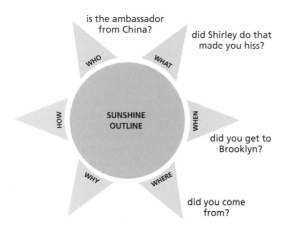

Questions for Shirley's Mother

▶ *Learning About Literature*

Point of View

"China's Little Ambassador" is written from the point of view of someone outside the story. The storyteller is not Shirley, her mother, her teacher, or a classmate. But the storyteller gives information that only Shirley would know.

This way of telling a story uses the "third person limited" point of view. It is "third person" because the teller is not one of the people in the story. It is limited — because the author uses only the facts that Shirley would know.

1. Look at the paragraphs in which Shirley tells her age. How old is Shirley in calendar years? How old does the principal think she is? What causes this confusion?
2. What other misunderstandings are there? Read some examples aloud to the class and discuss what caused them.
3. How do differences in culture lead to misunderstandings in real life? Describe a real-life example about someone who was misunderstood because of a difference in culture.

▶ *Writing*

Trying Out Points of View

Write about your first experience at school, some other first-time experience, or about a cultural misunderstanding. You can use the first-day-of-school chart you made earlier.

1. Write the story from your point of view. For example, "I came to Newcomer High School on October 5, 1992. I was very scared and shy. . . ."
2. Then write the story from someone else's point of view. For example, "James Chan came to our class at Newcomer High School on October 5, 1992. He didn't speak to anyone. We thought he didn't like us. . . ."

Unit Follow-Up

▶ Making Connections

Unit Project Ideas

Here are some possible unit projects. If you want, think up a project of your own. You can use some of the techniques you learned in this unit (word shaking, charting, drawing, and using sunshine outlines) to help you plan and complete your project.

1. Helping Newcomers. Do part or all of these activities.

Make a list that will help new students learn quickly about how things are done at your school. Explain some common misunderstandings (for example, how a student's age is determined or the order of first and last names in the United States). You can also translate the list into other languages.

If your school has video equipment, you can make a tape for new students that gives a tour of the school and describes its rules. The words can be English or another language.

2. Finding Other Songs About Beginnings. Find another song about beginnings. Bring in a recording or write out the lyrics to share with the class. Tell the class what the song means to you, if you wish.

3. Writing Song Lyrics. Make up a new verse to a song you like. It could be a song about new beginnings, such as "Here Comes the Sun."

4. Visual Art. Make a drawing, painting, or something else that tells about "beginnings." Write about how your artwork shows a new beginning.

5. Book of Symbols. Each person in your class or group can add to a book of symbols. These can be pictures drawn about ideas in this unit, or they can be cut out of magazines. Each person should write next to the symbol what it means to them.

You can put the pages together into a book. Add a title page, a table of contents, and your names.

Further Reading

Here are some books related to this unit that you might enjoy.

• *Aekyung's Dream,* by Min Paek. Children's Book Press, 1988. A wonderful dream helps a Korean girl adapt to her new culture. Written in both English and Korean.

• *The Beatles' Recording Sessions,* by Mark Lewisohn. Harmony Books, 1989. Studio session notes from 1962 to 1970 with photographs.

• *Homesick, My Own Story,* by Jean Fritz. G. P. Putnam's Sons, 1982. The author of many well-known books for young people tells about growing up a U.S. citizen in China and of going home.

• *How My Parents Learned to Eat,* by Ina R. Friedman. Houghton Mifflin, 1987. A young girl tells how her parents, an American sailor and a Japanese schoolgirl, met.

• *How They Became the Beatles: A Definitive History of the Early Years,* by Gareth L. Pawlowski. E. P. Dutton, 1989. Photographs tell the story of the Beatles from teenagers looking for places to play in 1960 to world-famous singers in 1964.

• *I'm in Charge of Celebrations,* by Byrd Baylor. Charles Scribner's Sons, 1986. Baylor, with artist Peter Parnall, celebrates special events in the desert, such as "Rainbow Celebration Day" and "The Time of the Falling Stars."

• *In the Year of the Boar and Jackie Robinson,* by Bette Bao Lord. Harper & Row, 1984. Shirley Temple Wong, a young Chinese girl, is at first confused but then adjusts to Brooklyn, New York, in 1947.

• *Onion John,* by Joseph Krumgold. Thomas Y. Crowell, 1987. A young boy begins an unusual friendship with an immigrant hobo.

• *Talking to the Sun,* edited by Kenneth Koch and Kate Farrell. Holt, Rinehart & Winston, 1985. This beautiful book includes poems from around the world for young people and art from the Metropolitan Museum of Art in New York.

The Starry Night by Vincent Van Gogh, 1889

People from all cultures
wonder how the world
was formed and how
things became the way
they are. This unit looks
at how several different
groups of people view the
origins of the world.

▶ *Exploring Your Own Experience*

Chants in Our Lives

Chants are poems with rhythm and repetition that people sing or say. People all over the world use chants in play, in prayer, and in meditation. The songs that Byrd Baylor wrote about in "The Way to Start a Day" are chants for prayer or meditation.

Many children recite chants as part of their play. The following is a North American chant used to choose the leader of a game. The words in the first and last lines are nonsense words—they don't mean anything. (One child walks around a circle of children, touching one person as he or she says each word. The person he or she points to on the last word is "the leader.")

> Eeny, meeny, miney, mo;
> Catch a tiger by the toe.
> If he hollers, let him go!
> Eeny, meeny, miney, mo.

Think of rhymes or chants from your childhood and share them with the class. Share them in any language, but try to use English to tell classmates what the chants mean.

▶ *Background*

Songs, stories, and chants are important parts of Navajo life. For hundreds of years, they have helped the Navajo pass on the values and history of their people. Winter—from first frost to last frost—is storytelling time for the Navajo. This serious chant tells the Navajo story of the first man and woman on earth.

There Are No People Song

Navajo Chant

You say there were no people.
Smoke was spreading over the earth.
You say there were no people.
Smoke was spreading.

First Man was the very first to emerge,
they say,
Smoke was spreading.
He brought with him the various robes and
precious things, they say,
Smoke was spreading.
He brought with him the white corn and
the yellow corn, they say,
Smoke was spreading.
He brought with him the various animals and
the growing things, they say,
Smoke was spreading.

---

spreading enlarging or expanding to cover more space
emerge come out
various different

Sunrise on Tioga Pass, High Sierra, California by Galen Rowell, 1973

You say there were no people.
Smoke was spreading.

First Woman was the very first to emerge,
they say,
Smoke was spreading.
She brought with her the various precious
things and robes, they say,
Smoke was spreading.

....

precious costly, dear, expensive

She brought with her the yellow corn and
the varicolored corn, they say,
Smoke was spreading.
She brought with her the various animals and
the growing things, they say,
Smoke was spreading.

You say there were no people.
Smoke was spreading.
You say there were no people.
Smoke was spreading.

---

varicolored many-colored

ABOUT THE NAVAJO

Because this is an ancient chant, it has no known author. The Navajo passed down this chant by telling it to others. In cultures where many or all people could not read or write, storytellers learned long stories and histories to pass along to younger family members. Since each storyteller changed the story a little, and since the names of the storytellers were not passed down, there is usually no known author for these types of stories.

The Navajo Indians are the largest group of Native Americans in the United States today. Their lands include parts of Arizona, New Mexico, and Utah.

▶ *What Do You Think?*

Think about the chant and discuss your ideas with your classmates and teacher. Here are some other ideas and questions to talk about.

1. What did First Man and First Woman bring with them? Is there a difference between First Man and First Woman? Find lines from the chant to show this.
2. What do you think "smoke was spreading" means? Why do you think it is repeated so many times?
3. Does the chant say that plants and animals came to earth before men and women? Is this like other stories you know about the beginning of the earth?
4. What are the main ideas in the chant? What items in the chant are repeated? What does this tell you about what is important to the Navajo?
5. How do you think the world got started? Where did plants and animals and people come from? What ideas in the chant do you agree with? What do you disagree with?

▶ *Try This*

Choral Reading

A choral reading occurs when two or more people read a poem, a story, or a play out loud. Some of the words in the chant you just read are in normal type, and some are in italic type. Divide into two groups. Have people with higher voices read the words in normal type and people with lower voices read the words in italic type. When you have practiced several times, invite a visitor or another class to hear you perform the chant.

▶ *Learning About Literature*

What Is the Chorus or Refrain?

Many songs or poems are written or sung with a *chorus* or *refrain,* a part that is repeated after each new *stanza* or *verse.* The chorus often states the theme or main idea of the song or poem over and over again. Discuss the following:

1. Which part of "There Are No People Song" is the refrain?
2. What is the theme or main idea of this chant?
3. Can you think of some other chants, songs, or poems with refrains? What are their main ideas?

▶ *Writing*

Saving Stories and Songs in Writing

Many wonderful stories and songs have never been written down.

1. Ask family members to tell you rhymes and songs from their homelands. Write them down.
2. Ask a native English speaker to recite a rhyme, chant, or song that he or she remembers. Write it down.
3. If you can, record the person on tape so that you can play it over and over again as you write down the words. Share what you have written with classmates.

▶ *Five Myths*

The following five stories are myths—stories that people tell to explain why things are the way they are. All cultures have myths about such things as how the earth began, why the sun and the moon are in the sky, or how people found fire.

▶ *Exploring Your Own Experience*

Clustering

Clustering is an activity to help you get ideas for writing. Look at the sample cluster below. The writer puts the main idea in the middle and then adds other ideas around the main idea. Try clustering about the subject of the story you will read, "How the Earth Was Made."

1. Write your main idea (for example, "how the world began") in the middle. Draw a circle around it.
2. Write anything you think of relating to the main idea in other circles. Connect them to the main idea with a line.
3. Look at each idea around the main idea. Write what these ideas make you think of. Connect these words to the appropriate circle.
4. Share your cluster with the class.

When you are getting ready to write, don't worry about getting everything right. Just think of as many ideas as you can. Write down anything you think of. Don't worry about your spelling or grammar. You can correct spelling or grammar later.

▶ *Background*

The Onondaga

The Onondaga are a group of Native Americans who live in what is now central New York State. In about 1400, they joined with the Iroquois Confederacy, a group of five Native American nations. The writers of the United States Constitution took ideas from the government of the Iroquois.

The early Onondaga lived in longhouses made of wood and bark. They lived by hunting, gathering, fishing, and later farming. This is the story the Onondaga tell about the creation of the world.

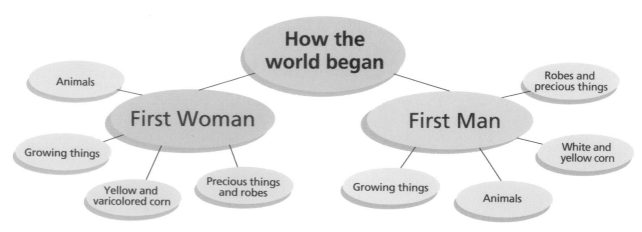

The Earth on Turtle's Back

retold by
Michael J. Caduto and Joseph Bruchac

BEFORE THIS EARTH EXISTED, there was only water. It stretched as far as one could see, and in that water there were birds and animals swimming around. Far above, in the clouds, there was a Skyland. In that Skyland there was a great and beautiful tree. It had four white roots which stretched to each of the sacred directions and from its branches all kinds of fruits and flowers grew.

There was an ancient chief in the Skyland. His young wife was expecting a child, and one night she dreamed she saw the Great Tree uprooted. The next day she told her husband the story.

He nodded as she finished telling her dream. "My wife," he said, "I am sad that you had this dream. It is clearly a dream of great power and, as is our way, when one has such a powerful dream we must do all we can to make it true. The Great Tree must be uprooted."

Then the Ancient Chief called the young men together and told them that they must pull up the tree. But the roots of the tree were so deep, so strong, that they could not budge it. At last the Ancient Chief himself came to the tree. He wrapped his arms around it, bent his knees and strained. At last, with one great effort, he up-

---

stretched reached out
the sacred directions the holy directions: north, south, east, and west
ancient very old

uprooted taken out of the ground
budge move

Swans by Joseph Stella, 1924–30

rooted the tree and placed it on its side. Where the tree's roots had gone deep into the Skyland there was now a big hole. The wife of the chief came close and leaned over to look down, grasping the tip of one of the Great Tree's branches to steady her. It seemed as if she saw something down there, far below, glittering like water. She leaned out further to look and, as she leaned, she lost her balance and fell into the hole. Her grasp slipped off the tip of the branch, leaving her with only a handful of seeds as she fell, down, down, down, down.

FAR BELOW, IN THE WATERS, SOME OF the birds and animals looked up.

"Someone is falling toward us from the sky," said one of the birds.

"We must do something to help her," said another. Then two Swans flew up. They caught the Woman From The Sky between their wide wings. Slowly, they began to bring her down toward the water, where the birds and animals were watching.

"She is not like us," said one of the animals. "Look, she doesn't have webbed feet. I don't think she can live in the water."

"What shall we do then?" said another of the water animals.

"I know," said one of the water birds. "I have heard that there is Earth far below the waters. If we dive down and bring up Earth, then she will have a place to stand."

So the birds and animals decided that someone would have to bring up Earth. One by one they tried.

The Duck dove first, some say. He swam down and down, far beneath the surface, but could not reach the bottom and floated back up. Then the Beaver tried. He went even deeper, so deep that all was dark, but he could not reach the bottom, either. The Loon tried, swimming with his strong wings. He was gone a long, long time,

....

grasping holding
glittering shining

but he, too, failed to bring up Earth. Soon it seemed that all had tried and all had failed. Then a small voice spoke.

"I will bring up Earth or die trying."

They looked to see who it was. It was the tiny Muskrat. She dove down and swam and swam. She was not as strong or as swift as the others, but she was determined. She went so deep that it was all dark, and still she swam deeper. She swam so deep that her lungs felt ready to burst, but she swam deeper still. At last, just as she was becoming unconscious, she reached out one small paw and grasped at the bottom, barely touching it before she floated up, almost dead.

WHEN THE OTHER ANIMALS SAW HER break the surface they thought she had failed. Then they saw her right paw was held tightly shut.

"She has the Earth," they said. "Now where can we put it?"

"Place it on my back," said a deep voice. It was the Great Turtle, who had come up from the depths.

They brought the Muskrat over to the Great Turtle and placed her paw against his back. To this day there are marks at the back of the Turtle's shell which were made by Muskrat's paw. The tiny bit of Earth fell on the back of the Turtle. Almost immediately, it began to grow larger and larger and larger until it became the whole world.

Then the two Swans brought the Sky Woman down. She stepped onto the new Earth and opened her hand, letting the seeds fall onto the bare soil. From those seeds the trees and the grass sprang up. Life on Earth had begun.

---

break the surface come up from under the water

Although myths have no known authors and have been passed down by word of mouth, people who write them down become the authors. Michael J. Caduto and Joseph Bruchac wrote down "The Earth on Turtle's Back."

Michael J. Caduto is an ecologist, author, and storyteller whose work has been featured on National Public Radio in the United States and on the British Broadcasting

Corporation. He learned about taking care of the environment from studying the culture of Native Americans and others who are rooted in the earth.

Joseph Bruchac is a poet, novelist, and storyteller from New York. His writings reflect his Native American (Abnaki) ancestry as well as the legends and lore of the Adirondack Mountains, where he was born.

▶ **Michael J. Caduto (born 1955)** ◀
▶ **Joseph Bruchac (born 1942)** ◀

▶ *What Do You Think?*

Think about the story and discuss your ideas with your classmates and teacher. Here are some other ideas and questions to talk about:

1. Why do you think the Ancient Chief pulled up the Great Tree? What else had to be given up so that there would be life on Earth?
2. Have you heard of the animals in these stories? Do you tell stories about animals in your culture? What animals? What happens to them?
3. Why do you think water animals are important in this Onondagan story?
4. Based on this story, can you guess other things that might be of importance to the Onondaga?

▶ *Learning About Literature*

The Elements of a Story

Many stories in English have the same elements or parts. Some of the main elements of stories are listed below.

the characters—the actors in the story

the setting—where and when the story takes place

the initial event—what happens to start the story

the reaction—what characters do when the first thing happens

the problem or goal—what the character(s) want to happen

the attempts to reach the goal—how the characters try to make it happen

the outcome—what happens when the characters try to reach their goal

the resolution—how things turn out in the end

▶ Try This

Story Mapping

A story map can help you to better understand a story. It is a chart or picture showing the main elements of a story.

Below is a sample story map of "The Earth on Turtle's Back." Some of the elements have been filled in. You can fill in the rest on your copy of the map.

▶ Writing

Using a Story Map for Prewriting

You can use a story map to get ready to write. It will help you remember the elements of a story. Use a blank story map to plan a story you would like to write. After you have made a story map, you can use it as a guide when you write and revise your story.

Story Map of "The Earth on Turtle's Back"

Story Elements

Characters	The Chief, the Sky Woman, the animals
Setting	
Initial Event	The Sky Woman had a dream.
Reaction	
Goal-setting	The animals decided she needed some land.
Attempt to Reach Goal	

▶ Four More Myths

The myths you are about to read all tell a basic story, such as how people came to have fire or how the sun and moon were created. The stories come from four different parts of the world, and they show how different cultures explained things in a way they understood.

▶ Exploring Your Own Experience

Myth Groups

An interesting way to study the four stories is by dividing into four groups. Each group will:

- Read and study one of the four myths.
- Make a story map of the myth.
- Prepare a short performance of the story for the class. One person can be the narrator, and the other people can act out the parts. Try to give each person something to say.
- Teach the class about the story by performing it as a skit or short play.
- Give encouraging responses to the performances. More suggestions about performing a skit appear at the end of the stories. Questions for discussing each story begin on page 70.

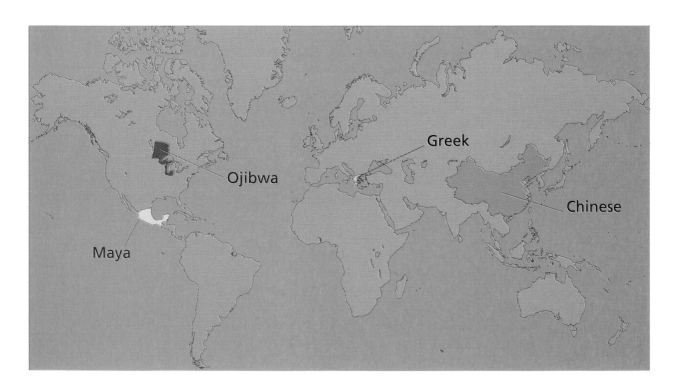

▶ Background

The Ojibwa

The Ojibwa lived in the cold region of present-day Ontario, Minnesota, northern Wisconsin, and northern Michigan in the "land of 10,000 lakes." In the summer, they lived in wigwams (tents) made from the branches and bark of trees. The cold winters made fire very valuable to the Ojibwa. Here is the story of how they first got fire.

The Chinese

China is a large country with many language and cultural groups. China has one of the oldest living civilizations, which goes back 3500 years. Chinese have long been famous for their fine arts and crafts. This story tells about Pan Ku, a craftsman who labored with a hammer and chisel to create the world.

Greek Myths

Hundreds of Greek myths, passed on by storytellers, tell of an age when gods, goddesses, and heroic figures walked the earth. Although the gods and goddesses never grew old and had amazing powers, they often acted like spoiled children: cheating, fighting, and becoming jealous. Prometheus is a hero who stole fire from the selfish gods to give to the people, and paid a high price.

The Mayans

The rich Mayan civilization grew and began to fade in the 1,000 years before Europeans set foot in the Americas. Between 300 and 900 B.C., the Mayans built pyramids and palaces and created beautiful sculptures and pottery in the lands that are now parts of Mexico, Guatemala, and Honduras. Fire was important in the slash and burn farming methods of the Mayans. Mayans, still proud of their language and heritage, tell this story about how fire came to their people.

The Fire Stealer

retold by
Pat Rigg

THIS IS THE STORY OF HOW THE Ojibwa got fire.

Long ago, the Ojibwa people in Canada had no fire. They had no fire to heat their homes, so they froze in the cold winters. They had no fire to cook their food, so they ate only raw meat and hard, raw vegetables. Without fire, life was very hard.

But an old, old man and his daughter who lived far, far away from the Ojibwa did have fire. They were warm in winter, and they ate warm, cooked meals. They refused to give any of their fire to the Ojibwa, even though they knew how the Ojibwa suffered in the cold Canadian winters.

The old people suffered the worst. One cold day a young Ojibwa boy named Nanabozho brought his old grandmother some meat, but she just shook her head and pushed it away. She was so old that she had lost many teeth and could not chew the tough, raw meat. She pulled her blanket closer around herself and bent her head down. Nanabozho looked at his old grandmother, cold and hungry, shivering in her blanket, and he knew he must do something. He decided to try to get some of the fire from the two who lived far away.

NANABOZHO WALKED MANY, MANY days. As he walked, he wondered how he could get close enough to the fire to steal some. He thought about the two people who had fire. How could he fool them? As he walked closer and closer to their home, he made a plan.

Finally he arrived at the house of the grandfather and the girl. The girl

---

raw uncooked
suffered withstood but not easily

tough hard to chew
shivering shaking from the cold
arrived got to

A Souteaux (Ojibwa) *Indian, travelling with his family in the winter near Lake Winnipeg* (c. 1825). Colored lithograph by H. Jones from a painting by Rendisbacher. Hudson's Bay Company Archives, Provincial Archives of Manitoba.

was outside working in the yard. Before she saw him, Nanabozho changed himself into a small rabbit. He hopped close to the girl, and she picked him up and petted him for a moment. When she went into the house, he hopped behind her and entered the house.

Then the grandfather came home. He saw the rabbit sitting under the table. "That rabbit belongs on the table," he said, "not under it. Grab him by the ears, slit his throat, and cook him for dinner." The girl picked up a sharp knife and came toward the rabbit. The rabbit took a giant jump toward the fire. As he jumped, Nanabozho quickly changed himself back into a boy. The girl and grandfather stared at him as Nanabozho grabbed a burning stick from the fire and ran.

Although they chased him, Nanabozho ran faster. As he ran, he touched the burning stick to the dry grass around him, and soon there was a field of fire between Nanabozho and his pursuers.

When Nanabozho reached home, he built a warm fire for his old grandmother and roasted meat and some grains. At last the old woman could eat.

Of course, Nanabozho and his grandmother shared the fire with the other Ojibwa. That is how the Ojibwa people got fire, and that is why today all Ojibwa homes are warm.

---

hopped jumped, ran like a rabbit

pursuers chasers

Pan Ku

retold by
Pat Rigg

CHINESE PEOPLE TELL A STORY about how Pan Ku made the world and sky, and how he corrected a mistake.

It was Pan Ku who made the earth. Pan Ku had a hammer and a chisel, and he worked with those tools, day after day, year after year, to create the world. At last Pan Ku finished his work. He had made a round sky and, inside it, a round earth. He put the first humans on the world and prepared to rest.

But the world was dark. Pan Ku had made a mistake—he forgot to put the sun and moon in the sky. The sun and the moon were hiding in the ocean. Everything was dark. Without the sun and moon, there was no light. Without the sun and moon there was no day or night. There was only darkness.

The first humans soon realized they needed the sun to make the day, and they needed the moon to make the night. The emperor of the first people sent word to the sun and moon: "Come out of hiding; come out of the ocean; come out and shine! We need the sun to make day; we need the moon to make night. Come out of hiding and work!" But the sun and moon stayed hidden in the ocean. There was no day; there was no night. The world stayed dark without one light.

---

chisel a sharp-edged tool pounded with a hammer to cut or shape wood, stone, or metal
prepared got ready

emperor ruler, king

Sun, Earth & Moon in Conjunction by Steven Hunt, 1991

The emperor called on Pan Ku: "Please help us. We have no day; we have no night. The sun and moon are hiding their light."

PAN KU HEARD THE EMPEROR, AND he realized his mistake. He had forgotten to put the sun and moon in the sky to give light and to make day and night.

So Pan Ku corrected his mistake. He drew a picture of the sun on one hand and drew a picture of the moon on his other hand. Then he stretched out his hands toward the ocean and spoke: "Come out of hiding; come out of the ocean; come out and shine! The sun will make day; the moon will make night. Come out of hiding and work." Seven times Pan Ku stretched out his hands to the sea and seven times he spoke these words: "Come out of hiding; come out of the ocean; come out and shine! The sun will make day; the moon will make night. Come out of hiding and work!"

The sun and moon heard Pan Ku and came out of hiding. They rode to the sky in chariots drawn by red dragons, and they began to work. The sun shone, and it was day. Then the moon shone, and it was night. Seven times the sun and moon alternated their light, and then they began again. They are still shining, still alternating day and night.

---

stretched out reached out

chariots two-wheeled carts pulled by horses and used long ago for war, racing, and parades
drawn pulled
alternating changing from one to the other

Prometheus

retold by

Pat Rigg

ONCE UPON A TIME PEOPLE HAD no fire to cook their food or warm their homes. A brave man stole fire from the gods and gave it to the people. His name was Prometheus. This is his story.

In ancient Greece, the gods lived on Mount Olympus and the Greek people lived below. The gods enjoyed the best of everything. They ate fresh bread and roasted lamb from their ovens; they listened to fine music and watched beautiful dancers. Fire made their homes warm and bright.

Down below Mount Olympus, the people had the worst of everything. They gnawed on hard, raw vegetables and chewed raw meat. Without fire they could not bake bread or roast meat. They shivered in the winter cold, even inside their small homes. Without fire, they could not warm or light their houses. In winter, they were too cold to make music or to dance in their cold, dark houses.

Prometheus looked up at Mount Olympus, and saw the gods feasting on fresh bread and roast lamb. Then he heard the music played for the dancers. He looked around him and saw the misery of his people. He determined he would ask the gods to give humans the gift of fire.

Prometheus climbed Mount Olympus, a very long and hard climb. He walked up the mountain for days, always thinking of how he could ask the gods for fire. After many days, he reached the home of the gods. Prometheus pleaded with the gods to

---

gnawed chewed

Attic red-figured Amphora (detail), c. 525 B.C.

give the gift of fire to people. He told them that giving this great gift would reduce human misery. He said that humans would thank the gods and would praise them for their benevolence. The gods discussed the idea among themselves. Some were in favor of giving fire to humans, but others were not. They feared that humans with fire might become as powerful as the gods. After a lengthy discussion, the gods told Prometheus that they would not give him fire. They told him to go back down the mountain.

PROMETHEUS PRETENDED TO RETURN but hid and waited until the gods were asleep. Then he left his hiding place and, very softly, walked to the fire and pulled out a burning stick. Quietly but quickly he ran away from the home of the gods. He ran as fast as he could to his own people. He gave the burning stick to them and told them how to keep the fire burning. He told them how to use the fire to cook food, to warm their homes and to make lights.

When the gods awoke that morning, they looked down at the people and saw smoke rising from many fires. The Greeks were cooking food—baking fresh bread, roasting lamb, boiling vegetables. They were warming themselves at their fires, and some were beginning to make a little music. The gods were furious. Prometheus had stolen their fire after they had refused to give him the gift. He had scorned the gods themselves.

His crime was great, so his punishment would be terrible. The gods punished Prometheus by chaining him to a rock on the mountain. Every day a black bird came to eat his liver; but every night the gods healed his liver so that Prometheus could not die. He would always suffer because he stole fire and gave it to the people.

---

benevolence kindness

awoke woke up, awakened
furious very angry
scorned rejected, looked down on, purposely ignored
liver organ inside the body near the stomach

How the Mayans Got Fire and Fooled Their Enemies

retold by

Aaron Berman

MANY, MANY YEARS AGO THE Mayans lived near a big lake. On the other side of the lake there was a different group of Indians. The two groups were enemies. The other group of Indians had fire and the Mayans didn't.

The Mayan chief wanted to get fire for his people. He knew that fire was very important for cooking and keeping warm.

He sent two of his men to ask the people on the other side of the lake for some of their fire. The men got in a boat and crossed the lake.

Those people wouldn't listen to the chief's men. They told them to leave and threw stones at their boats.

"Maybe they will be friendlier if I send them some gifts," the chief thought. He picked two other men and sent them across the lake. This time, the men took many beautiful and important gifts with them. They carried baskets of corn, beautiful hats with feathers, and blankets.

When they reached the other side of the lake, the people there were still not friendly. Again they told them to leave and threw stones at their boats.

The chief didn't know what to do. He spoke with all of the important men of his village.

They decided to steal some fire. This is how they did it. The Mayans had many dogs. The chief asked his

Mayan Seacoast Village, watercolor copy by Ann Axtell Morris of mural in Mayan Temple, A.D. 800–1000

people to find the most intelligent dog in the village. At last they found the dog. The chief put a stick in the dog's mouth and sent him across the lake.

The dog swam to the other side of the lake. It was nighttime when he arrived and everybody was sleeping.

The dog walked quietly to the fire in the center of the village and lit the stick.

No one saw him as he walked back to the lake. He swam across the lake very slowly because he didn't want the fire to go out. He swam so slowly that it took all night to cross the lake.

In the morning he reached his village and walked carefully to the chief. The chief took the stick and started a fire in the center of the village. That is the way the Mayans fooled their enemies and got fire.

---

intelligent smart

▶ *What Do You Think?*

Think about the four myths and discuss your ideas with your classmates and teacher. Sometimes you will want to go back to find examples to support your ideas. Several questions about each myth follow.

The Fire Stealer

1. Did the story make you feel sorry for anyone? Who? Why?
2. How does Nanabozho manage to steal fire?
3. How did he keep from getting caught?

Pan Ku

4. What mistake did Pan Ku make?
5. How did he correct his mistake?

Prometheus

6. Why didn't the gods want humans to have fire?
7. How did Prometheus plan to steal fire?
8. What happened to Prometheus after he stole the fire?

How the Mayans Got Fire and Fooled Their Enemies

9. How did the Mayans first try to get fire?
10. What did they do next?
11. How did they finally manage to get fire?

▶ *Try This*

Using Jigsaw Groups

A jigsaw is a puzzle in which all the parts fit together to make a whole. You can divide up a story as if it were a jigsaw puzzle. The members of the group can each become an expert in a small part of a story. Then, when they fit the pieces together, everyone understands the whole story. Here are the steps:

1. Divide a story into one part for each group member.
2. Each person becomes an expert on one part. To become an expert, study the story part very closely. Here are some ideas.

   • Look up words you don't know.
   • Draw pictures to illustrate your part.
   • Retell your part in your own words.
   • Act out your part of the story.

3. After you have become an expert, act out your part for the group.
4. After each person has presented a part, make a map of your story like the one you made for "The Earth on Turtle's Back."
5. Discuss what you think of the story.

▶ Learning About Literature

Using Readers' Theater

In Readers' Theater, one person reads a story while other people act out the roles and read the character's words. Sometimes it helps to tell the story in your own words and to give some of the narrator's parts to the characters.

Here is how "The Earth on Turtle's Back" might be changed into a Readers' Theater play. Read it, and act it out in your class.

The Earth on Turtle's Back for **Readers' Theater**

CHARACTERS
(In order of appearance)
Narrator
Swans
Duck
Beaver
Loons
Muskrat
Turtle
Great Tree
Sky Woman
Ancient Chief
Young Men

Narrator: In the beginning, there was only water, and in that water there were animals and birds swimming around.
(All the water animals and birds—the Swans, Duck, Beaver, Loons, Muskrat, and Turtle—swim around the stage and introduce themselves.)
Narrator: Far above, there was Skyland. In Skyland, there was a great tree. *(Tree takes a bow.)* There also was an Ancient Chief and his wife, Sky Woman, who was expecting a child. *(They walk on as they are introduced.)* One night, Sky Woman had a strange dream. The next morning, she told her dream to her husband.
Sky Woman: I had a strange dream last night. I dreamed that I saw the Great Tree uprooted.
Ancient Chief: My wife, I am sad that you

had this dream. It is clearly a dream of great power and, as is our way, when one has such a powerful dream we must do all that we can to make it true. The Great Tree must be up-rooted.

Narrator: So the Ancient chief called his young men to pull up the tree. But they could not budge it.

(Young Men try to uproot tree, but can't.)

So the Ancient Chief came to the tree and wrapped his arms around it. He bent his knees and strained. At last, he uprooted the tree. The tree left a great hole in the sky. Sky Woman leaned over to look down, grasping the tip of one of the Great Tree's branches. She leaned over too far, lost her balance, and fell into the hole. As she fell, she grasped the tip of the branch, leaving her with a handful of seeds.

(Sky Woman looks into an imaginary hole, and pretends to fall through the hole, grasping a branch.)

Sky Woman: Help, I'm falling!

Duck: Someone is falling toward us from the sky!

Muskrat: We must do something to help her!

Narrator: Two swans flying over the water saw her falling. They flew under her, close together, making a pillow for her to sit on. Gently, they began to bring her down toward the water.

(Swans cross hands to make a seat—woman sits on it.)

Beaver: She is not like us. Look, she doesn't

have webbed feet. I don't think she can live in the water.

Loon: What shall we do?

Duck: I know. I have heard that there is Earth far below the waters. If we dive down and bring up Earth, then she will have a place to stand.

Narrator: So the birds and animals decided that someone would have to bring up Earth. One by one they tried. Duck went down first, but he could not reach bottom. Then Beaver tried. She went even deeper, but she could not reach the bottom. Loon tried, swimming with his strong wings. Still no Earth.

Animals take turns diving down.

Narrator: Soon it seemed that all had tried and all had failed. Then a small voice spoke.

Muskrat: I will bring up Earth or die trying.

Narrator: It was tiny Muskrat. She was not as strong or as swift as the others, but she was determined. She went so deep that it was all dark, and still she swam deeper. She went so deep that her lungs felt ready to burst, but she swam deeper still. At last, just as she was be-coming unconscious, she reached out one small paw and grasped at the bottom, barely touching it before she floated up, almost dead.

Swans: Oh, no! She's dead!

Duck: No, I think she's still alive.

Beaver: But she has no Earth.

Loons: No, look! Her paw is closed, she has the Earth.

Muskrat: Now, where can we put it?

Turtle: Place it on my back.

Narrator: So they brought Muskrat over to the Great Turtle and placed her paw against his back. To this day there are marks at the back of the Turtle's shell that were made by Muskrat's paw. The tiny bit of Earth fell on the back of the Turtle. Almost immediately, it began to grow larger and larger and larger until it became the whole world.

Swans: Now we can put Sky Woman on the Earth.

Sky Woman: And I can plant these seeds from the Great Tree.

Narrator: From those seeds the trees and the grass sprang up. Life on Earth had begun.

▶ *Writing*

Writing and Performing Your Own Readers' Theater Play

Choose one of the myths, and rewrite it as a Readers' Theater play, using the play you just read as a model. Try to give everyone a speaking part. Practice telling the story and acting it out using costumes and props, if possible. Then present the play to the whole class.

Helping Other Students Perform

It's hard for almost everyone to get up and perform in front of the class. You can help your classmates learn by being a good audience member.

1. Applaud your classmates.
2. Encourage your classmates by telling them or writing to them about what you liked about their performance. You might compliment the following:

- the costumes or props
- the way the narrator read
- the actions or "business" of the characters
- the way someone spoke loudly and clearly or was easy to understand
- the way a group used music or scenery

The Readers' Theater

▶ *Exploring Your Own Experience* AM

Making a K/W Chart

Make a chart with two columns like the one below. At the top of one column, write "Know." At the top of the other column, write "Want to Know." Talk with your classmates about what you know about the moon and how it originated, or began. In the first column, write some of these things. In the second column, write things people in the class would like to know about the moon and how it originated.

▶ *Vocabulary*

What Do You Do with a New Word?

When reading nonfiction, you will often see words you don't know. Here are some ways to learn about the words.

1. First, read the whole sentence to see if you can get an idea about what the word means. Sometimes it is best if you don't stop reading to look up a word.
2. Then, if you still don't know what the word means and if you need the meaning to understand the paragraph, check the glossary at the bottom of the page or in the back of the book.
3. You may need to look in an English-English or a translation dictionary if you can't find the word in the glossary.
4. Write down new words and their meanings in your notebook for later study.

▶ *Background*

Writing about true events is called *nonfiction writing.* The following scientific article, which summarizes theories (best guesses based on scientific study) on how the Moon was formed, is nonfiction.

The Moon	
Know	*Want to Know*
It appears in the night sky.	*Where did it come from?*
	How long has it existed?

Birth of the Moon

by
Heather Couper and Nigel Henbest

THE SOLAR SYSTEM WAS BORN about 4,600 million years ago, as a swirling disc of gas and dust called a nebula. The big central "hub" became the Sun, while the outer regions of the disc condensed into the nine planets.

The oldest rock that the Apollo astronauts brought back was 4,600 million years old, so the Moon undoubtedly came into being at the same time as the Earth. According to one theory, the Moon was once part of the Earth, and split off because the Earth was rotating so rapidly. But the Apollo rock samples are rather different from the rock of the Earth's surface, so most astronomers have abandoned this idea.

The moons orbiting the other planets probably formed from swirling nebulae going around each planet like miniature Solar Systems. But in this case the Earth should have a family of moons, like those of Jupiter, not just

---

swirling going around and around

disc a round, flat shape, like a plate or a wheel

condensed changed from a gas or liquid to a solid, becoming smaller and heavier

undoubtedly without a doubt, definitely true

theory a scientist's guess based on facts and observations

rotating spinning, turning around

orbiting circling or moving around something

nebulae more than one nebula

Astronaut Edwin E. Aldrin, Jr. by Neil A. Armstrong, 1969

one Moon. In addition its orbit should not be tilted up, and the theory doesn't explain why the Moon's composition is different from the Earth's.

Other astronomers have suggested that the Moon formed as a planet in its own right, and that the Earth "captured" it when the Moon approached too closely. But it is difficult to explain how this capture occurred.

The latest theory explains the fact that the Moon's rocks are slightly different from the Earth's by the idea that a giant meteorite hit the Earth, and splashed out matter that later condensed into the Moon. In the process, some elements evaporated into space, so changing the composition of the Moon's rocks.

Three theories of the Moon's birth:

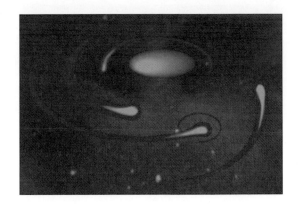

Nebula

When the Solar System formed from a giant swirling disc of gas and dust, individual whirls turned into the planets. The gases around each planet condensed into moons. Some planets acquired a system of moons, but the material around the Earth formed into a single Moon.

---

tilted slanted
composition what something is made of
captured took prisoner
occurred happened, came to be
meteorite rock from space
evaporated changed from solid or liquid to gas, as water when it boils

individual single, one at a time
system group in a pattern

Capture

The Moon formed as a separate planet, rather closer to the Sun than the Earth. The Moon's orbit crossed the path of the Earth—just as the orbit of Pluto crossed that of Neptune. When the Moon came too close, the Earth's gravity swung it around into an orbit around the Earth.

Moonsplash

A giant meteorite hit the Earth in its early days and splashed rock into space. Many of these rock fragments went into orbit as miniature moons, forming a ring around the Earth—rather like the rings of Saturn. These rocks gradually came together and built up into the Moon.

gravity the pull of the Earth which makes things fall back to Earth

fragments pieces

Heather Couper has been fascinated by space and the stars since childhood. Now a professional astronomer, she has written books and participated in TV and radio show broadcasts throughout the United Kingdom.

Nigel Henbest, colleague and friend of Heather Couper, is a writer, broadcaster, and consultant on astronomy. He has written books in his field, as well as articles for magazines, newspapers, and encyclopedias.

▶ **Heather Couper (born 1949)** ◀
▶ **Nigel Henbest (born 1951)** ◀

▶ *What Do You Think?*

Think about this article and discuss your ideas with your classmates and teacher. Here are some other ideas and questions to talk about.

1. Are scientists sure about the way the Moon was formed? Why or why not?
2. What are the three theories about the moon's formation?
3. What are the problems with these theories?
4. Which theory do you think best explains the formation of the Moon? Why?

▶ *Confirm*

"What You Knew" and "What You Wanted to Know"

Look back at the chart you made before you read this selection. Discuss these questions:

1. Did the selection agree with what you knew before?
2. Did you learn anything that you wanted to know?
3. Are there still some things you want to know?

How the Moon Was Formed

Main Ideas	*Details and Examples*
Theory 1 *Nebula*	*Nebula gases condensed to form moons. Earth got only one moon.*
Theory 2	
Theory 3	

▶ *Try This* **AM**

Double-Column Note-Taking

Learning to take good notes will help you to study better. Double-column notes will help you decide what is most important about what you have read. Then you will better understand and remember what you have read.

1. To take double-column notes, divide your paper into two columns. (See the example on the facing page.)
2. List the main ideas in the left-hand column. Often, ideas that authors think are important will be in headings or in bold-faced, dark type.
3. Put details about the main ideas in the right-hand column.

▶ *Writing*

To develop your understanding of one of the theories of how the Moon was formed, and to help your classmates understand it better as well, try this project:

- Work with a group of about four people.
- Choose one of the three theories to study.
- Try to find more pictures and information about the theory in a library.
- Make a model of what happened according to your theory. Use markers, paint, clay, dough, styrofoam, papier-mâché, or whatever materials you have available.
- Rewrite the theory in your own words.
- Explain your model and theory to the class. Make sure that each person in your group has something to say.

METEORITE THEORY

Unit Follow-Up

▶ Making Connections

Unit Project Ideas

Here are some possible unit projects. If you want, think up a project of your own. You can use some of the techniques you learned in this unit (for example, interviews, story mapping, jigsaw groups, and Readers' Theater) to help you plan and complete your project.

1. From Myth to Reality. In this unit you have read myths, which explain things in a nonscientific way, and scientific writing, which explains things based on facts.

Now, try to find ideas in myths that might be based on fact. For example, perhaps water animals existed before land animals, as in "The Earth on Turtle's Back."

a. Choose a myth to study from this unit, from your family, or from a library book.

b. Read the myth, and look for ideas that might be true.

c. Check an encyclopedia or science books to learn more about those ideas.

d. Write or tell your class about them.

2. Sewing the Unit Together with an Origins Quilt.

a. Each student makes a picture of some part of the unit. Try to make sure that each selection has at least one person making a drawing about it.

b. The first volunteer puts a picture on the wall and tells about it.

c. A second volunteer does the same.

d. The class looks at the two pictures and talks about how they are similar. For example, you might talk about how both pictures are about stories that tell how people got fire.

e. Then someone writes a sentence about the similarity on a strip of paper and tacks it on the wall to "sew" the pictures together. See the example on the facing page.

f. Continue until all the pictures have been sewn together into one big picture of the unit.

3. Practice Double-Column Note-Taking. Try out the double-column note-taking strategy in another class. Bring in your notes to show your ESL class. Tell your classmates how the strategy helped you.

4. Just-So Stories: Class Book of Origins. Each person can use the writing process to write a short story about how something came to be the way it is. You might write about topics like these:

why ducks have flat feet
why zebras have stripes
why the sky is blue

After your writing is edited, illustrate it. Combine all of the stories in a class book.

5. New Words Dictionary. Start your own dictionary of words you want to learn. Use a spiral notebook, and write one letter of the alphabet on each page. When you find a new word you want to remember, write it on the page with the word's first letter. Use a translation, an English definition, and/or a picture to help you remember the meaning. Study your dictionary for a few minutes each day.

Further Reading

Here are some books related to this unit that you might enjoy.

• *D'Aulaires' Book of Greek Myths,* by Ingrid and Edgar Parin D'Aulaires. Doubleday & Company, Inc., 1980. Classic stories of gods and heroes, with pleasing illustrations.

• *Favorite Folktales from Around the World,* by Jane Yolen. Pantheon Books, 1988. Over 160 delightful stories from five continents.

• *Forestville Tales,* by Aaron Berman. Heinle & Heinle, 1977. Eight folk tales from various cultures in an easy-to-understand text.

• *In the Beginning: Creation Stories from Around the World,* by Virginia Hamilton. Harcourt, Brace and Jovanovich, 1988. Creation myths from around the world.

• *Keepers of the Earth: Native American Stories and Environmental Activities,* by M. J. Caduto and J. Bruchac. Fulcrum, Inc., 1988. Each Native American story is followed by activities to help readers interact with and understand the natural environment.

• *Today's World: Planet Earth,* by Douglas Dixon. Gloucester Press, 1989. Text and illustrations describe the formation of the planet Earth and its evolution to its present state.

Double Dutch Series: Keeping Time by Tina Dunkley, 1986

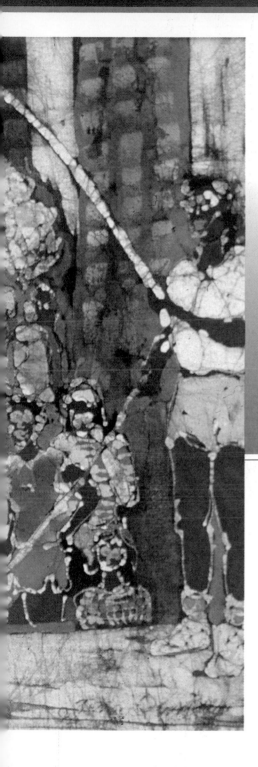

What makes a good friendship? Do friends need to be alike, or can they be very different? Does it take time for a friendship to grow, or can it happen quickly? This unit explores and tries to help you discover what friendship is.

▶ *Exploring Your Own Experience*

Paired Dialogues About Friends

Work with a partner. Choose a problem that is important to both of you. Choose opposite sides of the problem, and write down your conversation. Keep writing until you reach a solution. Share your dialogue with the class. The sample below will get you started.

▶ *Background*

Sometimes friendships take a long time to develop. *Driving Miss Daisy* is a play about the growing friendship between an elderly white woman and her African-American chauffeur (driver) over a 25-year period. This friendship is one of a kind because Daisy and Hoke are so different—they are of different gender, different race, different age, different religions, and different social class.

This selection contains two scenes from the play. At the beginning, the playwright (author of a play) lists the cast of characters, or people who appear in the play, in the order in which they appear. Stage directions describe the actions of the characters and are printed in *italic type.*

Hoke's words are written in a southern black English dialect. Many words are similar to standard English. *Jes'* means "just"; *Miz* means "Miss" or "Mrs."; *Yassum* means "Yes, ma'am." You will be able to understand such terms by reading the whole sentence in which they appear.

Problem: A friend wants you to help her cheat on a test.

Marie:	*Hey, Sandra! Come sit next to me for the algebra test!*
Sandra:	*Thanks, Marie, but I think I'll sit here.*
Marie:	*But I went out last night and didn't study. I need you!*
Sandra:	*I don't know, Marie . . .*

Driving Miss Daisy

by
Alfred Uhry

CHARACTERS:

Daisy Werthan: *A widow* (age 72–97)
Hokc Coleburn: *Her chauffeur* (age 60–85)
Boolie Werthan: *Her son* (age 40–65)
Time and Place: *This play takes place from 1948 to 1973, mostly in Atlanta, Georgia. There are many locales. The scenery is meant to be simple and evocative.*

Daisy is a 72-year-old retired schoolteacher. When she wrecked her car in her own driveway, her son, Boolie, insisted that she get a chauffeur to drive for her. She did not like the idea, and was sure that she would not like Hoke, the chauffeur. Daisy and Hoke, a man of great humor, patience, and dignity, have learned to respect and appreciate one another over time despite their many differences. But they don't talk about their growing friendship. As the scene opens, Miss Daisy is taking care of the flowers on her dead husband's grave.

evocative bringing out a mental picture
grave place where a dead person is buried

Scene One

Lights come up brightly, indicating hot sun. Daisy, in a light dress, is kneeling, a trowel in her hand, working by a gravestone. Hoke, jacket in hand, sleeves rolled up, stands nearby.

Hoke: I jes' thinkin', Miz Daisy. We bin out heah to the cemetery three times dis mont' already and ain' even the twentieth yet.

Daisy: It's good to come in nice weather.

Hoke: Yassum. Mist' Sig's grave mighty well tended. I b'lieve you the best widow in the state of Georgia.

Daisy: Boolie's always pestering me to let the staff out here tend to this plot. Perpetual care they call it.

Hoke: Doan' you do it. It right to have somebody from the family lookin' after you.

Daisy: I'll certainly never have that. Boolie will have me in perpetual care before I'm cold.

Morgan Freeman as *Hoke* in the movie *Driving Miss Daisy*

Hoke: Come on now, Miz Daisy.

Daisy: Hoke, run back to the car and get that pot of azaleas for me and set it

---

trowel garden tool for digging

ain' ain't, isn't

widow a woman whose husband has died

pestering bothering

perpetual care when people pay cemetery owners to take care of graves forever

Doan' Do not

lookin' after (looking after) taking care of

before I'm cold before my body gets cold when I die

azaleas flowering shrubs that bloom in the spring in the South

on Leo Bauer's grave.

Hoke: Miz Rose Bauer's husband?

Daisy: That's right. She asked me to bring it out here for her. She's not very good about coming. And I believe today would've been Leo's birthday.

Hoke: Yassum. Where the grave at?

Daisy: I'm not exactly sure. But I know it's over that way on the other side of the weeping cherry. You'll see the headstone. Bauer.

Hoke: Yassum.

Daisy: What's the matter?

Hoke: Nothin' the matter.

He exits. She works with her trowel. In a moment Hoke returns with flowers.

Miz Daisy . . .

Daisy: I told you it's over on the other side of the weeping cherry. It says Bauer on the headstone.

Hoke: How'd that look?

Daisy: What are you talking about?

Hoke (*deeply embarrassed*)**:** I'm talkin' 'bout I cain' read.

Daisy: What?

Hoke: I cain' read.

Daisy: That's ridiculous. Anybody can read.

Hoke: Nome. Not me.

Daisy: Then how come I see you looking at the paper all the time?

Hoke: That's it. Jes' looking. I dope out what's happening from the pictures.

Daisy: You know your letters, don't you?

Hoke: My ABCs. Yassum, pretty good. I jes' cain' read.

Daisy: Stop saying that. It's making me mad. If you know your letters then you can read. You just don't know you can read. I taught some of the stupidest children God ever put on the face of this earth and all of them could read enough to find a name on a tombstone. The name is Bauer. Buh buh buh buh Bauer. What does that buh letter sound like?

Hoke: Sound like a B.

Daisy: Of course, Buh Bauer. Er er er er er. Bau-*er*. That's the last part. What letter sounds like er?

Hoke: R?

Daisy: So the first letter is a—

Hoke: B.

Daisy: And the last letter is an—

Hoke: R.

---

weeping cherry cherry tree with long branches that hang down like tears
headstone marker on someone's grave
embarrassed ashamed

Nome No, ma'am
dope out figure out

Daisy: B-R. B-R. B-R. Brr. Brr. Brr. It even sounds like Bauer, doesn't it?

Hoke: Sho' do Miz Daisy. Thass it?

Daisy: That's it. Now go over there like I told you in the first place and look for a headstone with a B at the beginning and an R at the end and that will be Bauer.

Hoke: We ain' gon worry 'bout what come in the middle?

Daisy: Not right now. This will be enough for you to find it. Go on now.

Hoke: Yassum.

Daisy: And don't come back here telling me you can't do it. You can.

Hoke: Miz Daisy . . .

Daisy: What now?

Hoke: I 'preciate this, Miz Daisy.

Daisy: Don't be ridiculous! I didn't do anything. Now, would you please hurry up? I'm burning up out here.

Light goes out on them.

Scene Two

(Boolie and his wife Florine are planning a Christmas party. Daisy is displeased because the family is Jewish and she thinks they shouldn't be celebrating a Christian holiday.)

In the dark we hear Eartha Kitt singing "Santa Baby." Light up on Boolie. He wears a tweed jacket, red vest, holly in his lapel. He is on the phone.

Boolie: Mama? Merry Christmas. Listen, do Florine a favor, all right? She's having a fit and the grocery store is closed today. You got a package of coconut in your pantry? Would you bring it when you come? *(He calls off stage)* Hey, honey! Your ambrosia's saved! Mama's got the coconut! *(Back into the phone)* Many thanks. See you anon, Mama. Ho ho ho.

Lights out on Boolie and up on Daisy and Hoke in the car. Daisy is not in a festive mood.

Hoke: Ooooooh at them lit-up decorations!

Daisy: Everybody's giving the Georgia Power Company a Merry Christmas.

Hoke: Miz Florine's got 'em all beat with the lights.

Daisy: She makes an ass out of herself every year.

Hoke *(Loving it)*: Yassum.

Sho' do It sure does
ridiculous very laughable

holly leaves used to make wreaths
having a fit very upset
ambrosia dessert made with oranges and coconut
anon later

Daisy: She always has to go and stick a wreath in every window she's got.

Hoke: Mmm-hmmm.

Daisy: And that silly Santa Claus winking on the front door!

Hoke: I bet she have the biggest tree in Atlanta. Where she get 'em so large?

Daisy: Absurd. If I had a nose like Florine I wouldn't go around saying Merry Christmas to anybody.

Hoke: I enjoy Christmas at they house.

Daisy: I don't wonder. You're the only Christian in the place!

Hoke: 'Cept they got that new cook.

Daisy: Florine never could keep help. Of course it's none of my affair.

Hoke: Nome.

Daisy: Too much running around. The Garden Club this and the Junior League that! As if any one of them would ever give her the time of day!

But she'd die before she'd fix a glass of ice tea for the Temple Sisterhood!

Hoke: Yassum. You right.

Daisy: I just hope she doesn't take it in her head to sing this year. *(She imitates)* Glo-o-o-o-o-o-o-o-o-o-o-o-o-oriaaaa! She sounds like she has a bone stuck in her throat.

Hoke: You done say a mouthful, Miz Daisy.

Daisy: You didn't have to come. Boolie would've run me out.

Hoke: I know that.

Daisy: Then why did you?

Hoke: That my business, Miz Daisy. *(He turns into a driveway and stops the car)* Well, looka there! Miz Florine done put a Rudolph Reindeer in the dogwood tree.

Daisy: Oh my Lord! If her grandfather, old man Freitag, could see this! What is it you say? I bet he'd jump up out of his grave and snatch her bald-

---

wreath circle of leaves or branches people put on their doors and windows at Christmas time

Santa Claus Father Christmas; bearded man in red suit said to bring Christmas gifts

absurd foolish, silly

they their

the Garden Club neighborhood organization for women

the Junior League service organization for women

Temple Sisterhood service club run by Jewish women

done say a mouthful said something true and important

run me out given me a ride

Morgan Freeman as *Hoke* and Jessica Tandy as *Daisy* in the movie *Driving Miss Daisy*

headed!

Hoke opens the door for Daisy.

Wait a minute. *(She takes a small package wrapped in brown paper from her purse)* This isn't a Christmas present.

Hoke: Nome.

Daisy: You know I don't give Christmas presents.

Hoke: I sho' do.

Daisy: I just happened to run across it this morning. Open it up.

Hoke *(Unwrapping package)*: Ain' nobody ever give me a book. *(Laboriously reads the cover)* Handwriting Copy Book—Grade Five.

Daisy: I always taught out of these. I saved a few.

Hoke: Yassum.

Daisy: It's faded but it works. If you practice, you'll write nicely.

Hoke *(Trying not to show emotion)*: Yassum.

---

laboriously with lots of work
emotion feeling

Daisy: But you have to practice. I taught Mayor Hartsfield out of this same book.

Hoke: Thank you, Miz Daisy.

Daisy: It's not a Christmas present.

Hoke: Nome.

Daisy: Jews don't have any business giving Christmas presents. And you don't need to go yapping about this to Boolie and Florine.

Hoke: This strictly between you and me. They seen us. Mist' Werthan done turn up the hi-fi.

Daisy: I hope I don't spit up.

Hoke takes her arm and they walk off together as the light fades on them.

---

yapping talking (like a noisy little dog)

▶ *What Do You Think?*

Think about the play, and discuss your ideas with your classmates and teacher. Here are some questions to think about and discuss:

Scene One

1. Where and when does the play take place (the setting)?
2. What happens there (the action)?
3. How does the playwright (author of a play) describe the setting and action?
4. Do you think Daisy knew Hoke couldn't read? What lines from the play make you think so?
5. How do you think Hoke felt when he told Daisy he couldn't read? What lines from the play show this?
6. How does Daisy show that she respects Hoke's feelings?
7. What kind of person is Daisy?
8. What kind of person is Hoke?
9. What do the characters do and say that tell you what they are like?
10. Do you know any people who can't read or who can't read English? How do you think they feel?

Scene Two

11. How does Daisy feel about her son and his wife? How do you know?
12. Why is Daisy concerned that someone might find out that she gave a Christmas present to somebody?
13. How can you tell that Daisy and Hoke are friends? Which lines show you this?

14. Why do you think the two became friends, instead of remaining just employer and worker? How do you think they overcame all of their differences?

▶ *Try This*

Compare and Contrast Characters AM

A Venn diagram uses circles to show similarities and differences between topics. A sample Venn diagram appears below. It compares and contrasts dogs and cats. Notice that some things describe only dogs, some things describe only cats, and some things describe both dogs and cats.

Now make a Venn diagram to compare and contrast Hoke and Daisy. In one circle, put words and phrases that describe Daisy. In the other circle, put words and phrases that describe Hoke. In the place where the circles overlap, put words and phrases that describe both characters.

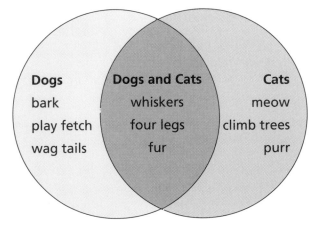

Dogs	Dogs and Cats	Cats
bark	whiskers	meow
play fetch	four legs	climb trees
wag tails	fur	purr

▶ Learning About Literature

Comparing Drama and the Short Story AM

A genre is a kind of literature. In this book, you have already seen four genres: poems ("The Way to Start a Day"), short stories ("China's Little Ambassador"), myths ("The Earth on Turtle's Back"), and nonfiction ("Birth of the Moon"). *Driving Miss Daisy* is a play. The genre is called *drama.* It tells a story like a short story does, but it is written for people to act out before an audience.

- The playwright uses stage directions—shown in italic type in the play—to tell the actors what to do.
- The words are written as speeches by the characters, with the name of the character who is talking at the beginning of the line.

Make a chart like the one below comparing *Driving Miss Daisy* with "China's Little Ambassador."

- How do the words look on the page?
- Who is telling the story?
- How is the setting described?
- How are the actions shown?
- How do you learn about the characters?

▶ Writing

Dialogues

Look at the dialogue you wrote before reading *Driving Miss Daisy*. Using this play as a model, rewrite the dialogue as a short play. Include a title, the author's name, the setting, the characters, and stage directions. Write the speaker's name with a colon (:) before each speech.

Point of Comparison	Drama	Short Story
How do the words look on the page?	There is a list of people in the play at the beginning. A new line begins every time a different person speaks.	Text arranged in paragraphs. Dialogue shown by quotation marks. A new line starts when a new person talks.
Who is telling the story?		

▶ *Exploring Your Own Experience*

What Is a Friend?

Think about someone who is a good friend. Write down words and phrases that describe how you like your friends to act. Compare your list to other people's lists, and discuss what the most important qualities of a friend are.

▶ *Background*

Following are two poems. One is a Chinese poem from the first century B.C. by an anonymous (unknown) author. The other is a U.S. song from the 1960s. In both, the speaker promises to be a good friend.

In many countries, words are formed by combining letters of the alphabet to form words. But in China, where our next selection is from, words are formed by combining nearly 50,000 characters. For example, these two characters combine to mean "friendship." This type of writing is called calligraphy, which means "beautiful handwriting."

Oath of Friendship

Anonymous

Shang Ya!
I want to be your friend
For ever and ever without
break or decay.
When the hills are all flat
And the rivers are all dry,
When it lightens and thunders
in winter,
When it rains and snows
in summer,
When Heaven and Earth
mingle—
Not till then will I part from
you.

....

mingle mix together

Untitled by Keith Haring, 1985

Bridge Over Troubled Water

by
Paul Simon

When you're weary,
feelin small,
When tears are in your eyes,
I'll dry them all;
I'm on your side.
Oh, when times get rough
And friends just can't be found

Like a Bridge Over Troubled Water
I will lay me down.
Like a Bridge Over Troubled Water
I will lay me down.

---

weary tired
rough difficult

Red Boardwalk by Mike Mazzaschi, StockBoston

When you're down and out,
When you're on the street,
When evening falls so hard
I will comfort you.
I'll take your part.
Oh, when darkness comes . . .
And pain is all around,

Like a Bridge Over Troubled Water
I will lay me down.
Like a Bridge Over Troubled Water
I will lay me down.

....

down and out feeling bad; without money or a job

Sail on silver girl,
Sail on by.
Your time has come to shine.
All your dreams are on their way.
See how they shine.
Oh, if you need a friend
I'm sailing right behind.

Like a Bridge Over Troubled Water
I will ease your mind.
Like a Bridge Over Troubled Water
I will ease your mind.

ABOUT THE SONGWRITER

Paul Simon is a U.S. singer, guitar player, and composer of popular music. Many people have praised him for the poetry of his songs. He and Art Garfunkel formed an important folk-rock duo in the 1960s called *Simon and Garfunkel*.

Simon is now a solo performer who often works with musicians from other cultures. In his hit albums *Graceland* and *Rhythm of the Saints*, Simon has used Latin American, South African, and other multicultural artists.

▶ **Paul Simon (born 1942)** ◀

▶ *What Do You Think?*

Think about the song and poem, and discuss your ideas with your classmates and teacher. Here are some questions you can consider:

1. Who is speaking in the poem and the song?
2. What kind of friend is described in each?
3. How do these friends compare with your ideas from the activity you did before reading?
4. What are the times when we most need friends? What examples does the poet write about?
5. How do the poet and the songwriter describe good times and bad times?
6. How do they describe lasting friendship?

▶ *Try This*

Bridges

Think about the pictures that went through your mind as you read the poem and the song. Draw a picture that shows what you saw, and write a one-sentence caption under the picture. Share your work with others to find out what the poem and song meant to them.

I'll be there when you need me.

► Learning About Literature

Imagery

When a writer describes something in a way that is so real that you can see, hear, smell, feel, or taste it in your mind, that writer is using *imagery.*

A writer can use words to create a picture in your mind. For example,

"When the hills are all flat
And the rivers are all dry, . . .
Not till then will I part from you."

"When tears are in your eyes,
I'll dry them all."

Simile

Another way to create an image is to use a *simile*—a comparison using the word *like* or *as.* Here are some examples of similes:

"Like a Bridge Over Troubled Water
I will ease your mind."

"She is as sly as a fox."

Can you find similes in other poems, songs, or sayings?

Try to write some similes. Use one or both of these patterns if they help:

A friend is like _____.
A friend is as _____ as _____.

Metaphor

Still another way to create an image is to use a metaphor. In a metaphor, you compare one thing to another without using *like* or *as.* You say that something is something else. "My friend is a bridge over troubled water" or "She is a sly fox" are metaphors.

Write some metaphors. Use this pattern if it helps:

A friend is _____.

► Writing

Friendship Poetry

Write about having a friend or being a good friend.

Suggestions:

- Use ideas and terms from the semantic map your class made.
- Use some of the similes and metaphors you wrote.
- Use this pattern to write several lines:
  When _____ I will _____.
- Or use this pattern:
  I will be your friend until _____.

▶ Exploring Your Own Experience

Do a Quickwrite

A quickwrite is an activity to help you experience the fun and pleasure of writing. To do this, write your thoughts as they come. Write without stopping, trying to get all of your ideas down. Follow these steps:

1. Choose one of the following quotes.
   "One only understands the things that one tames."
   "One must observe the proper rites."
   "It is only with the heart that one can see rightly; what is essential is invisible to the eye."
   "You become responsible, forever, for what you have tamed."

2. For 5–10 minutes, write everything that comes into your head about the saying. You can correct grammar, spelling, and punctuation later.

3. When you finish writing, share your work with someone else who wrote about the same quotation.

4. Read your quickwrites aloud to one another, and discuss your different ways of viewing the quotation.

5. Write down a group summary of your quickwrites.

▶ Background

The Little Prince is a fantasy (a story that could not happen in real life) written by Antoine de Saint-Exupéry. In the story, a pilot's airplane breaks down over the Sahara Desert. He is left to make repairs a thousand miles from any other human. He is visited by a little prince from outer space, who tells the pilot about his adventures. One of these adventures involves the little prince's conversation with a fox about the meaning of friendship.

The Fox

from
The Little Prince
by Antoine de Saint-Exupéry

I T WAS THEN THAT THE FOX appeared.

"Good Morning," said the fox.

"Good morning," the little prince responded politely, although when he turned around he saw nothing.

"I am right here," the voice said, "under the apple tree."

"Who are you?" asked the little prince, and added, "You are very pretty to look at."

"I am a fox," the fox said.

"Come and play with me," proposed the little prince. "I am so unhappy."

"I cannot play with you," the fox said. "I am not tamed."

"Ah! Please excuse me," said the little prince.

But, after some thought, he added:

"What does that mean—'tame'?"

"You do not live here," said the fox. "What is it that you are looking for?"

"I am looking for men," said the little prince. "What does that mean—'tame'?"

"Men," said the fox. "They have guns, and they hunt. It is very disturbing. They also raise chickens. These are their only interests. Are you looking for chickens?"

"No," said the little prince. "I am looking for friends. What does that mean—'tame'?"

---

tame make something wild into something domesticated, as one tames an animal to be a pet

Little Prince illustration by Antoine de Saint-Exupéry, 1943

"It is an act too often neglected," said the fox. "It means to establish ties."

" 'To establish ties'?"

"Just that," said the fox. "To me, you are still nothing more than a little boy who is just like a hundred thousand other little boys. And I have no need of you. And you, on your part, have no need of me. To you, I am nothing more than a fox like a hundred thousand other foxes. But if you tame me, then we shall need each other. To me, you will be unique in all the world. To you, I shall be unique in all the world . . ."

"I am beginning to understand," said the little prince. "There is a flower . . . I think that she has tamed me."

"It is possible," said the fox. "On the Earth one sees all sorts of things."

"Oh, but this is not on the Earth!" said the little prince.

The fox seemed perplexed, and very curious.

"On another planet?"

"Yes."

"Are there hunters on that planet?"

"No."

"Ah, that is interesting! Are there chickens?"

"No."

"Nothing is perfect," sighed the fox.

But he came back to his idea.

"My life is very monotonous," he said. "I hunt chickens; men hunt me. All the chickens are just alike, and all the men are just alike. And, in consequence, I am a little bored. But if you tame me, it will be as if the sun came to shine on my life. I shall know the sound of a step that will be different from all the others. Other steps send me hurrying back underneath the ground. Yours will call me, like music, out of my burrow. And then look: you see the grain-fields down yonder? I do not eat bread. Wheat is of no use to me. The wheat fields have nothing to say to me. And that is sad. But you have hair that is the color of gold. Think how wonderful that will be when you have tamed me! The grain, which is also golden, will bring me back the thought of you. And I shall love to listen to the wind in the wheat . . ."

---

neglected left out, not done
establish make, set up, start
unique like no other
perplexed confused, not understanding

monotonous boring; the same thing over and over again
in consequence as the effect of some cause

The fox gazed at the little prince, for a long time.

"Please—tame me!" he said.

"I want to, very much," the little prince replied. "But I have not much time. I have friends to discover, and a great many things to understand."

"One only understands the things that one tames," said the fox. "Men have no more time to understand anything. They buy things all ready made at the shops. But there is no shop anywhere where one can buy friendship, and so men have no friends anymore. If you want a friend, tame me . . ."

"What must I do, to tame you?" asked the little prince.

"You must be very patient," replied the fox. "First you will sit down at a little distance from me—like that—in the grass. I shall look at you out of the corner of my eye, and you will say nothing. Words are the source of misunderstandings. But you will sit a little closer to me, every day . . ."

The next day the little prince came back.

"It would have been better to come back at the same hour," said the fox. "If, for example, you came at four o'clock in the afternoon, then at three o'clock I shall begin to be happy. I shall feel happier and happier as the hour advances. At four o'clock, I shall already be worrying and jumping about. I shall show you how happy I am! But if you come at just any time, I shall never know at what hour my heart is to be ready to greet you. . . . One must observe the proper rites . . ."

"What is a rite?" asked the little prince.

"Those also are actions too often neglected." said the fox. "They are what make one day different from other days, one hour from other hours. There is a rite, for example, among my hunters. Every Thursday they dance with the village girls. So Thursday is a wonderful day for me! I can take a walk as far as the vineyards. But if the hunters danced at just any time, every day would be like every other day, and I should never have any vacation at all."

So THE LITTLE PRINCE TAMED THE fox. And when the hour of his departure drew near—

"Ah," said the fox, "I shall cry."

---

rites important ceremony usually done the same way each time, such as wedding or funeral rites
departure leaving

Little Prince illustration by Antoine de Saint-Exupéry, 1943

"It is your own fault," said the little prince. "I never wished you any sort of harm; but you wanted me to tame you . . ."

"Yes, that is so," said the fox.

"But now you are going to cry!" said the little prince.

"Yes, that is so," said the fox.

"Then it has done you no good at all!"

"It has done me good," said the fox, "because of the color of the wheat fields." And then he added:

"Go and look again at the roses. You will understand now that yours is unique in all the world. Then come back to say goodbye to me, and I will make you a present of a secret."

THE LITTLE PRINCE WENT AWAY, TO look again at the roses.

"You are not at all like my rose," he said. "As yet you are nothing. No one has tamed you, and you have tamed no one. You are like my fox when I first knew him. He was only a fox like a hundred thousand other foxes. But I have made him my friend, and now he is unique in all the world."

And the roses were very much embarrassed.

"You are beautiful, but you are empty," he went on. "One could not die for you. To be sure, an ordinary passerby would think that my rose looked just like you—the rose that belongs to me. But in herself alone she is more important than all the hundreds of you other roses: because it is she that I have watered; because it is she that I have put under the glass globe; because it is she that I have sheltered behind the screen; because it is for her that I have killed the caterpillars (except the two or three that we saved to become butterflies); because it is she that I have listened to, when she grumbled, or boasted, or even sometimes when she said nothing. Because she is *my* rose.

AND HE WENT BACK TO MEET THE fox.

"Goodbye," said the fox. "And now here is my secret, a very simple secret: It is only with the heart that one can see rightly; what is essential is invisible to the eye."

"What is essential is invisible to the eye," the little prince repeated, so that he would be sure to remember.

"It is the time you have wasted for

---

essential very important or necessary
invisible not able to be seen

your rose that makes your rose so important."

"It is the time I have wasted for my rose—" said the little prince, so that he would be sure to remember.

"Men have forgotten this truth," said the fox. "But you must not forget it. You become responsible, forever, for what you have tamed. You are responsible for your rose . . ."

ABOUT THE AUTHOR

Antoine de Saint-Exupéry was a novelist, essayist, and pioneering aviator. After serving in the French Air Force, he helped establish airmail routes over northwest Africa, the South Atlantic, and South America.

His literary works, many based on his piloting experience, portray the heroic adventures of early aviators. During World War II, Saint-Exupéry disappeared while flying a reconnaissance mission over occupied France.

▶ Antoine de Saint-Exupéry (1900–1944) ◀

▶ *What Do You Think?*

Think about the story, and discuss your ideas with your classmates and teacher. Here are some questions to think about and discuss:

1. What does being tamed mean to you? Are you tamed by your friends? Are they tamed by you?

2. Find the following quotations in the text.

   "One only understands the things that one tames." (p. 108)

   "One must observe the proper rites." (p. 108)

   "It is only with the heart that one can see rightly; what is essential is invisible to the eye." (p. 110)

   "You become responsible, forever, for what you have tamed." (p. 111)

   • Read the parts before and after the quotes.

   • Find out who said the quotation and what was happening when it was said.

   • Discuss what you think each quotation means. Compare your responses after reading the story with your responses beforehand.

3. Find another interesting quotation from the story. Read it aloud to a group of classmates. Share your ideas, and ask others to give you their views about what your quotation means.

▶ *Try This*

Theme Statement

Write one short sentence that summarizes what this selection means to you. Make an attractive poster with that sentence to display in the classroom. Add artwork, if you wish.

▶ Learning About Literature

Theme Statements

The theme of a work is the writer's message about human nature or the meaning of life. Look at the sayings from "The Fox" and at the posters your class made. Do you think that any of them tell the theme of this story? Do you have other ideas about what the theme might be? Try to state the themes of other selections in this unit.

▶ Writing

Dialogue

"The Fox" is almost entirely dialogue; the story is told through the words of the little prince and the fox. Look at the text to see how Saint-Exupéry uses paragraphs, commas, and quotation marks to show who is speaking:

"Goodbye," said the fox. "And now here is my secret, a very simple secret: It is only with the heart that one can see rightly; what is essential is invisible to the eye."

"What is essential is invisible to the eye," the little prince repeated, so that he would be sure to remember.

The following rules are used by Saint-Exupéry and other writers when writing dialogue.

- Put quotation marks before and after someone's exact words.
- Start a new paragraph every time a different person speaks.

- Use a comma after someone's words (and before the quotation mark) if the sentence doesn't end when the person stops talking. If the sentence ends, use a period.

1. Find other examples of how Saint-Exupéry follows these rules in "The Fox."
2. Talk with several classmates about things you like to do. Write down or tape-record a short (about one minute) segment of your conversation. Write out the dialogue you hear according to the rules just given.

Examples:

Mai said, "I love to go shopping."

"I never want to see her again," said Gina.

"I just got a new job," he said excitedly.

▶ *Exploring Your Own Experience*

Round Table

A hero or heroine is a person whom people admire because he or she has been very brave and has done something important to help others. In small groups, take turns writing the answers to these questions:

1. Can you tell a true story about someone who was a hero or heroine? If yes, briefly tell your story.
2. What would you do if someone started shooting in your neighborhood?

▶ *Background*

This selection is a nonfiction article that appeared in a magazine. It tells about a Boston man who was injured while protecting two neighborhood children from gunfire.

A Brave Man Lays His Life on the Line

by
Joe Treen and S. Avery Brown

Morlan O'Bryan heroically saves two children—but may never walk again.

APRIL 26 WAS A WARM SPRING evening, and a dozen residents of Capen Green, a new subdivision in the Dorchester section of Boston, were out in front of their houses enjoying the weather. Suddenly five teenagers came running around the corner chased by four others. One of the neighbors, Susan Stephen, spotted the danger first. "Guns!" she screamed. "They've got guns!"

As shots rang out, everyone ducked for cover; some, like Morlan O'Bryan, 33, threw themselves on the ground. Then O'Bryan looked up. He saw Stephen's two children—Nebulla, 9, and Joseph, 6, running directly into the line of fire. O'Bryan didn't hesitate. He dove for the youngsters, turning himself into a human shield. But as he pushed Nebulla under his front stairs, he felt "a kick in my back." He had been hit by a 9-mm. bullet—a bullet that he believes would have struck Nebulla in the head. "It buckled my legs," he says. "I went right down to the ground."

---

subdivision a small planned neighborhood in which the houses were built at about the same time
spotted saw
ducked for cover got down behind something

line of fire the line between the gun and the target; the path of the bullet
buckled to become weak and bend

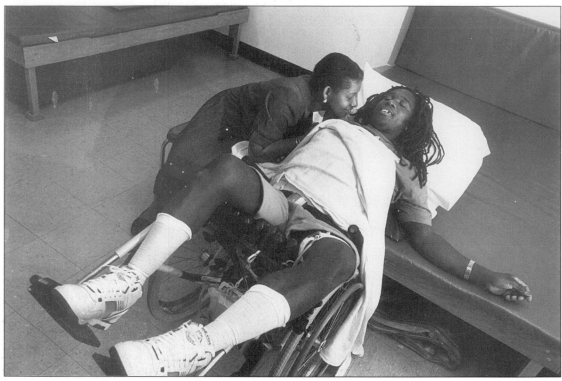

Morlan O'Bryan with wife Loudalia by Stella Johnson/People Weekly

O'Bryan was the only one in Capen Green hurt that night. The bullet pierced his lower back, injuring his spinal cord. It is not clear if he will ever walk again. Virtually everyone, from Nebulla and Joseph Stephen to Boston Mayor Raymond Flynn, has told him he is a hero. But Morlan, the father of five young children (ages 2 to 11), doesn't see it that way. "Sure," he says, "I'm proud of what I did. But it was what any father would do. I was just trying to help two little kids, that's all."

virtually nearly, almost completely

To have done nothing, he adds, would have been worse. "If I had left those two kids and they got shot," he says, "it would have been like a living hell." Remarkably, he harbors no ill will toward the street toughs, still at large, who shot him. "Forgiveness is better," he says. "Those kids don't know nothing about family, the love of a father. If I could talk to them, I would tell them to put down their guns and stop killing."

---

harbors has; holds
ill will bad feelings

at large free; not caught by the police

ABOUT THE AUTHORS

Sue Avery Brown started writing at the age of fifteen in her home state of Connecticut. Now, she lives south of Boston by the ocean. Although she has written articles on many different topics as a freelance writer, her favorite stories are about real people's lives.

Joe Treen lived in many cities as a child, including Chicago, Milwaukee, Houston, and St. Louis. Today, he lives in the New York City area with his wife who is also a professional writer. He has been a freelance writer for many publications such as *Newsweek, The Boston Globe,* and *Newsday.*

▶ **S. Avery Brown (born 1947)** ◀
▶ **Joe Treen (born 1942)** ◀

▶ *What Do You Think?*

Think about the article, and discuss it with your classmates and teacher. Below are some questions to discuss.

1. What do you think of Morlan O'Bryan? Would you have acted the way he did? Is he angry at the people who hurt him? Would you be?

2. How do you think the writers of this story learned about Morlan O'Bryan? What people are quoted in the article? Why do you think the writers used so many quotations in writing this story?

▶ *Try This*

Events in a Narrative—Cause and Effect

A narrative is writing that tells a story.

Events in a story can be related by cause and effect. Why something happened (the event that happened first) is the cause, and the change that takes place is the effect. Make a chart showing the events that were causes and the events that were effects in this article.

1. Try to remember the main events that happened in this article. Have one person write down the events as others remember them.

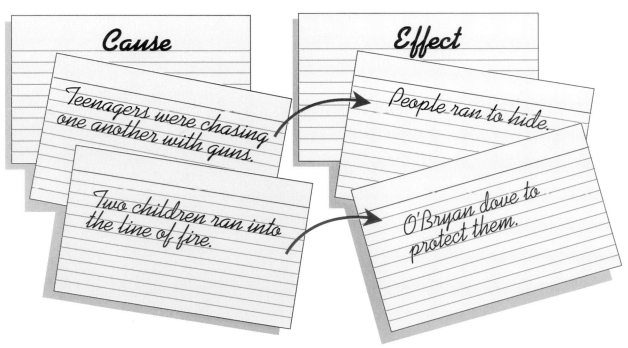

Cause

Teenagers were chasing one another with guns.

Two children ran into the line of fire.

Effect

People ran to hide.

O'Bryan dove to protect them.

2. Write each event on a separate index card.
3. Make one card that says "Cause" and another that says "Effect" and create one pile for each.
4. Put the events that were causes into the first pile under the "Cause" card. Put the events that were effects into the second pile, next to the events that caused them.
5. Some things that were effects will also cause the next event. Make another card for these events to put in the cause pile.
6. Use the sample on the facing page to get you started.

▶ *Learning About Literature*

Reading and Writing a Magazine Article

Good writers do a lot of legwork (going to people to get firsthand information) to write an article like this one. Often they try to get information from many people about an event so they can describe what really happened.

- Newspaper and magazine articles usually have a strong opening. The first paragraph gets your attention and makes you want to read the rest.
- Newspaper and magazine articles contain the important facts. The article answers these news questions: Who? What? When? Where? Why? How?

- Newspaper and magazine articles put most of the main information in the first few paragraphs. This is for two reasons: (1) people who read articles sometimes don't have time to read the whole thing; and (2) editors often have to cut articles to fit the space they have, and they usually cut from the end.

Can you find the 5 W's and H (who, what, when, where, why, and how) in the first two paragraphs of this article? Use a sunshine outline (see page 16) to check.

▶ *Writing*

Newspaper or Magazine Writing AM

Work with a partner to research an article about a real event in your school or neighborhood in which someone was (or was not) a good friend or neighbor. Talk to several people who saw the event and make notes or tape recordings. Get the answers to the basic facts: who, what, when, where, why, and how.

Write the article, revise it with your peers, and edit it with your teacher. Make sure you have a good lead, information from several sources, and all of the important facts.

Compile the articles into a class newspaper, or submit them to your school or neighborhood newspaper.

Unit Follow-Up

▶ Making Connections

Here are some possible unit projects. If you want, think up a project of your own. You can use some of the techniques you learned in this unit (writing dialogues, making Venn diagrams, using similes and metaphors, or doing a quickwrite) to help you plan and complete your project.

Unit Project Ideas

1. What Is a Friend? Unit Chart. Make a chart to compare and contrast friendship from the point of view of characters and authors in the unit. Add a column that tells what you think. See the example below.

2. A Letter to a Friend. Is there someone far away that you want to keep in touch with? Is there someone across the street who has been a good friend? Write, revise, and send a letter or postcard to a friend or to a pen pal you hope will become a friend. See the example on the facing page.

3. Friendship: The Book. Compile your articles on people who have been good friends and neighbors into a class book.

4. Being a Friend: The Play. Make a play or video about friendship. You can use or adapt one of the selections from the unit, or a dialogue or poem you wrote. If you prefer, you may write a new skit. Share the completed performance with another class.

Selection	Character	View on Friendship	My View
Driving Miss Daisy	Daisy	A friend helps another friend learn to read.	A friend helps me learn English.
Driving Miss Daisy	Hoke	A friend is there even at times when it's not easy, like holidays.	A friend is a friend all of the time, not just when it's easy.

Further Reading

Here are some books related to this unit that you might enjoy.

- **Best Friends,** edited by Lee Bennet Hopkins. Harper & Row, 1986. Langston Hughes, Prince Redcloud, and others contribute eighteen short poems on friendship.

- **Bridge to Terabithia,** by Katherine Patterson. HarperCollins, 1977, 1987. Two outsiders form a special friendship and create their own magical kingdom.

- **Driving Miss Daisy,** by Alfred Uhry. Theatre Communications Group, Inc., 1988. Over the years, an elderly Southern Jewish woman and her black chauffeur become friends.

- **A Gathering of Old Men,** by Ernest Gaines. Knopf, 1983. A man is killed. A woman and a dozen old men claim to have killed him to protect someone they care about.

- **The Little Prince,** by Antoine de Saint-Exupéry. Harcourt Brace Jovanovich, 1971. A fantastic prince travels around the universe making friends and learning about life.

- **My Best Friend Duc Tran,** by Diane MacMillan and Dorothy Freeman. Julian Messner/Simon & Schuster, 1987. Vietnamese-American culture and customs are presented through a fictional story.

- **My Brother Sam Is Dead,** by James Lincoln Collier and Christopher Collier. Macmillan, 1984. During the American Revolution, a boy has to choose between fighting his father on one side and his brother on the other.

- **The Outsiders,** by S. E. Hinton. Dell, 1968. Gang members learn about friendship and the importance of life.

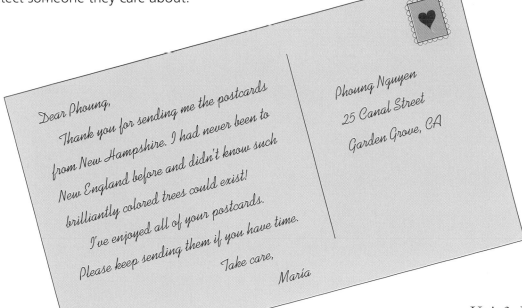

Dear Phoung,

Thank you for sending me the postcards from New Hampshire. I had never been to New England before and didn't know such brilliantly colored trees could exist! I've enjoyed all of your postcards. Please keep sending them if you have time.

Take care,
María

Phoung Nguyen
25 Canal Street
Garden Grove, CA

The Swimmer in the Aquarium by Henri Matisse, c.1944

4

Wishes and Dreams

All people have wishes, dreams, or hopes for the future. The selections in this unit explore wishes and dreams in many genres and from several points of view.

▶ *Exploring Your Own Experience*

Fortune Telling AM

Every day we wish for things. We use words such as "want," "need," and "hope" to express our wishes. Share a wish with a partner. Then play a fortune-telling game using two playing cards, one with red print and one with black print. Mix up the cards so you don't know which one is which, and place them face down on the desk. Take turns with yes-or-no questions and then pick up a card. Black means "yes," and red means "no."

▶ *Background*

All of us have dreams, wishes, or desires for the future. The two poems by Langston Hughes explore what happens when dreams are held on to or dreams are lost.

Dreams

by
Langston Hughes

Hold fast to dreams
For if dreams die
Life is a broken-winged bird
That cannot fly.

Hold fast to dreams
For when dreams go
Life is a barren field
Covered with snow.

barren empty

California Gulls, Mono Lake, California by Galen Rowell, 1974

Dream Deferred

by
Langston Hughes

What happens to a dream
deferred?

Does it dry up
like a raisin in the sun?

Or fester like a sore—
And then run?

---

deferred put aside until later, postponed
fester become infected
sore wound; injury; hurt place

That Gentleman by Andrew Wyeth, 1960

Does it stink like rotten meat?
Or crust and sugar over—
like a syrupy sweet?

Maybe it just sags
like a heavy load.

Or does it explode?

....

crust and sugar over form a hard sugar
surface
sags hangs down

ABOUT THE AUTHOR

Langston Hughes, a well-known African-American poet, was born in Missouri and traveled a great deal. He is perhaps best known for his poems about the lives of African Americans in Harlem, in New York City. His poems reflect the rhythms of African-American speech and music, especially jazz.

▶ **Langston Hughes (1902–1967)** ◀

▶ *What Do You Think?*

1. How does each poem make you feel? Why? What is the mood of each poem?
2. Sometimes sentences tell a fact, and other times sentences ask questions. What kinds of sentences does each poem use?
3. What are some of the words or phrases used to describe dreams in the poems?
4. Do you think one poem uses stronger, more powerful words? Which one? What are the words?
5. What dreams of your own do you hang on to? What dreams have you given up? What dreams might you give up one day?

▶ *Learning About Literature*

How Poets Appeal to Our Senses

Poets often appeal to our senses of sight, hearing, taste, touch, and smell. Look back at these two poems, and find examples of how Hughes appeals to your senses. Make a chart like the one below, and fill it in with examples from the poems. Share your completed chart with a partner.

Sense	Examples
Sight	a broken-winged bird that cannot fly
Hearing	
Taste	
Touch	
Smell	

▶ *Try This*

A Class Poem

1. Make up sentences that begin with the words "A dream come true . . ." Choose words that appeal to the five senses (seeing, hearing, feeling, tasting, smelling), the way Langston Hughes did. For example, "A dream come true is hearing my name called at graduation."

2. Write the sentences on the board.

3. Work in groups of four. Choose some sentences on the board and turn them into questions. For example, "Is it a dream come true to hear my name called at graduation time?"

4. Combine the questions into a class poem. Read the poem together, and suggest ways to rearrange the lines so they sound better. Post the final poem in the classroom, or put it in a class book of poems.

▶ *Writing*

Sense Poems

Write your own poem about your dreams, wishes, observations, or some other topic. Try to include at least one line that appeals to each sense.

▶ *Exploring Your Own Experience*

Wish Stories and Symbols

In North America children often make wishes on the first star they see at night, reciting this rhyme:

Star light, star bright
First star I see tonight,
I wish I may, I wish I might
Have the wish I wish tonight.

Many objects are used for wishing. The chart below shows two examples. Other objects or symbols commonly used for wishes or good luck include: rainbows, wishing wells, fountains, lost teeth, birthday candles, and a rabbit's foot.

Choose one of these objects or another that your family or friends use for wishes or good luck. Draw the object and write a description of how it is used. Share your writing with friends and revise it. Combine all of the drawings and descriptions from the class into a book or bulletin-board display.

▶ *Background*

Many cultures have stories in which wishes are granted through magic. Discuss stories you remember in which a magic object, person, or animal makes wishes come true.

Object	*How it Brings Good Luck*
Four-leaf clover	*You will have good luck or a wish come true if you find one.*
Wishbone	*Save the forked bone in the front of the breastbone of a chicken or turkey and dry it. Two people grasp the bone from opposite ends, make a wish, and pull. The bone will break. The person who gets the larger bone piece will have a wish granted.*

The Carpenter's Son

by

Mohammed Reshad Wasa

translated by Abdul Haq Walahs

ONCE, A LONG TIME AGO, THERE was a boy named Salim. His father, who had been a carpenter, was dead. The boy and his mother were very poor and for many years they lived from hand to mouth.

One day, Salim's mother managed to raise a little money by selling her husband's chisel and saw. She gave the money to Salim, saying: "Son, you're grown now. So take this money and go into business with it."

With the money in his pocket, Salim went to the bazaar. There he met a man who had a cat for sale. Using all the money, he bought the cat and took it home.

Salim's mother was astonished. "Here we can hardly feed ourselves," she said. "So how can we feed a cat as well?"

A few days later the mother sold her husband's old shoes. She gave the money to Salim and said: "Buy something better this time."

At the bazaar Salim met a man who had a dog for sale. Again he used all the money and brought the dog home.

His mother was still more upset. "Wasn't a cat enough!" she exclaimed.

A few days later she sold her last possession, an old rug. She gave Salim the money, saying: "Salim, this is our last hope. There's nothing more left to

---

lived from hand to mouth (idiom) were very poor; only had enough food for one meal at a time
chisel and saw tools for working with wood
bazaar a market or street of shops or stalls

astonished very surprised
as well also, too
possession something one owns

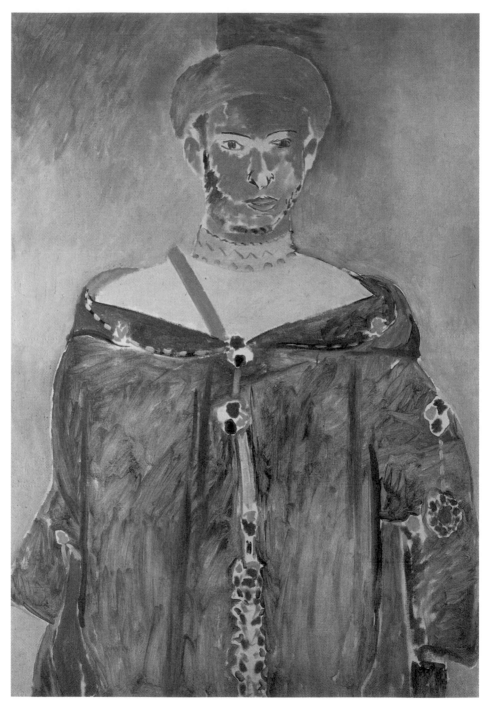

Ruffian Standing by Henri Matisse, 1912

sell. Get something useful this time."

This time at the bazaar Salim met a man with a snake that had a brightly colored crown on its head. Again he spent all his money and brought the snake home.

His mother was frightened. "What do you mean by spending our last money on a snake?" she cried. "At least the cat catches mice and the dog guards our hut, but what good is a snake? Take it out at once and kill it."

Salim took the snake outside. But when he was about to hit it with a rock, the snake spoke. "Ah, kindhearted one," it said to Salim, "please don't kill me. I'm the son of the King of Snakes. Take me back to my father's palace, and he'll reward you richly."

Salim agreed, and on the way the snake said: "When we get to the palace, my father will ask you what reward you want. Don't ask for anything except the ruby my father carries in his mouth. It's not only the largest and most brilliant of all his jewels, but whoever possesses it will have all his wishes fulfilled."

The King of Snakes was very pleased to have his son safely back. He thanked Salim deeply and promised to give him whatever he wanted.

"There's only one thing I want," said Salim, "and that's the ruby you keep in your mouth."

The king was taken aback. "No, I can't give you the ruby," he said. "Ask for anything else and I'll give it to you."

Again Salim asked for the ruby, and again the king refused. Salim was about to leave the palace without any reward, when the king's son spoke: "Father, Salim saved my life and you promised him anything he wanted. If you won't keep your promise, I'm going to leave too."

The king could not bear to lose his son again; so he gave Salim the ruby.

Salim returned home to his mother with the magic jewel. Then he wished for food and clothes and a better house to live in. No sooner had he made his wishes than he saw their old hut turn into a mansion. He and his mother were wearing beautiful new

---

hut small house, shack
ruby red precious stone
brilliant shining bright
fulfilled caused to be or happen, granted, come true

taken aback (idiom) surprised, shocked
mansion large home of very rich person

clothes, and before them there was a table loaded with all kinds of delicious foods and costly wines.

FROM THAT DAY ON, SALIM AND HIS mother had everything they wanted. One day Salim happened to see the daughter of the king and fell in love with her. As was the custom of the land, Salim sent his mother to ask the king to let his daughter marry her son. But when the king heard that Salim was only a carpenter's son, he refused.

Salim sent his mother to the palace a second time to tell the king that, even if he was only a carpenter's son, he could give the king anything he wanted.

The king laughed and said: "If your son will build me a new palace made of bricks of gold and silver, then I'll give him my daughter for his bride."

The mother brought this message to her son, who made the wish on his ruby. Next morning, when the king awoke, he was amazed to see a beautiful new palace, next to his own, made of gold and silver bricks. So the king kept his promise, and Salim married the princess.

Thereafter Salim lived in the new palace with his beautiful wife, his old mother, the cat, and the dog. One day when he was out hunting he saw an old woman crying bitterly beside a grave. He asked her what was the matter, and she told him she had just lost her only son and had no one to look after her. So the kindhearted Salim felt pity and invited her to come and live in the palace. What he did not know was that the old woman was actually an evil witch who had heard about his ruby and wanted to steal it.

ONE DAY, WHILE SALIM WAS AWAY, the old woman asked the princess how Salim had become so wealthy, and the princess told her about the magic ruby.

"May I have just one look at it?" the witch asked. When the princess said she didn't know where her husband kept the ruby, the witch exclaimed: "You don't know! Aren't you his wife?" Then she said, in a whisper: "My dear, you must find out how much your husband loves you. Ask him for the ruby. That will be a true test of his love for you."

When Salim returned, the princess asked him to prove his love by giving her the ruby. He answered: "I love you more than all the treasures of the

loaded full of
costly expensive

world." Giving her the ruby, he warned: "But you must guard it very carefully."

The princess showed the ruby to the witch and then locked it away carefully in her jewel box. But no locks were safe against the witch. One night when everyone had gone to sleep, she easily opened the box and stole the ruby. Then she wished on the ruby that the palace would disappear and that Salim's wife and mother should be cast away in distant villages.

When Salim woke up, there was no sign of the palace, nor of his wife and mother. Only his dog and cat remained by him. Feeling very sad, he walked out into the country, followed by the cat and dog. Searching for the jewel, they traveled day and night, hungry and thirsty, passing through many towns and villages. Finally Salim was too tired to go on. But the two faithful animals continued the search for the ruby.

One day the two animals came to a place where a wedding was about to be celebrated. It was the wedding of the son of the King of Rats. Salim's cat caught the rat prince and told him that he would not free him unless the other rats found the magic ruby. Thousands of rats scurried everywhere, and finally a lame rat found the house of the old witch. She was asleep with the jewel gleaming in her mouth. The rat sprinkled some snuff on his tail and flicked it under the witch's nose. She sneezed so hard that the jewel was thrown out of her mouth. Leaping into the air, the rat caught the ruby and fled. Then he brought it to the cat, who finally freed the rat prince.

THE CAT AND DOG BEGAN THEIR journey back to Salim. Along the way they came to a wide river. The dog gave the cat a ride on his back and began to wade across the river, while the

---

cast away thrown away

scurried ran around
lame disabled, having a hurt leg or foot
gleaming shining
snuff a form of smokeless tobacco
flicked moved quickly
leaping jumping
fled ran away
wade walk in shallow water

Sarah on the Terrace by Henri Matisse, 1912

cat held the ruby in his mouth. Halfway across the river, the cat saw a delicious-looking fish swimming by. Forgetting everything, the cat opened his mouth to speak to the dog—and out the jewel popped. It fell right into the fish's mouth, and the fish disappeared into the water.

How the dog scolded the cat for his carelessness! Day after day the two animals sat there by the river, wondering how to recover the ruby. Then one day the cat saw a fisherman pulling up out of the river a fish whose skin was gleaming with a strange red light. This must be the fish who had swallowed the ruby! Swiftly, the cat leaped upon the fish and ripped it open. There was the ruby gleaming in the fish's stomach.

Again the cat and the dog set out on their journey. This time the dog carried the ruby. He ran as fast as he could, with the cat following. Salim was near death when they finally reached him. He was so delighted to see his faithful dog and cat, and so overjoyed to have the ruby back, that

he became well at once. He told the jewel to bring back his palace, with his wife and mother in it. Immediately he found himself in the palace with his loved ones. They kissed one another joyfully and shed tears of happiness.

His wife and mother told him how unhappy they had been because of the witch's treachery. Salim ordered the witch to be brought to him. He said to her: "You've been very cruel to all of us. I'll give you one of two choices: do you want a whip or a horse?"

The old witch answered: "Naturally, I'd prefer the horse."

So Salim had a horse brought. He had his men tie the witch to the horse's tail. Then they whipped the horse, which ran out of the palace and then went galloping across the countryside dragging the old witch behind him.

Thus Salim rid himself of the evil witch forever, and thereafter he and his wife and mother lived happily in the palace, together with the faithful dog and cat.

---

scolded criticized, spoke angrily to
ripped it open tore it open
overjoyed very happy

shed tears cried
treachery trickery
thereafter after that

▶ *When Did It Happen?*

Form small groups. Work together to write the following sentences on a sheet of paper in the right order. Check the story to be sure.

- Salim meets the evil witch.
- Salim's mother sells the shoes, and Salim buys a dog.
- Salim lives happily ever after with his wife, his mother, the dog, and the cat.
- The witch steals the ruby.
- The witch is punished.
- Salim's mother sells the rug, and Salim buys a snake.
- Salim's mother sells the chisel and saw, and Salim buys a cat.
- Salim returns home with the magic jewel.
- The snake offers Salim a reward.
- The cat and dog bring the ruby back to Salim.
- Salim marries the princess.

▶ *What Do You Think?*

This story is a folktale, a story passed on by telling it out loud. Folktales often teach values or show which values and beliefs are important in a culture. How do you think the tellers of this story would answer the questions that follow? Try to find evidence in the story to support your view and discuss it in class.

1. Is lying OK sometimes, or should you always tell the truth?
2. Is it OK to waste money on things you don't need?
3. Is being a loyal friend important?
4. How should a person treat parents or children?
5. Is it OK to break a promise sometimes?
6. Is it better to be poor or rich?

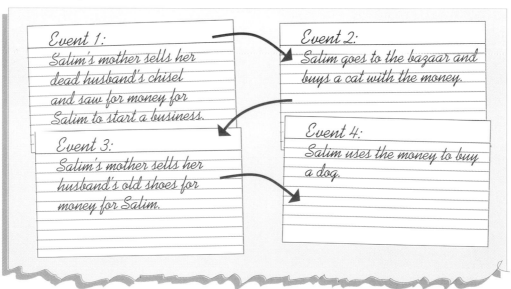

Event 1:
Salim's mother sells her dead husband's chisel and saw for money for Salim to start a business.

Event 2:
Salim goes to the bazaar and buys a cat with the money.

Event 3:
Salim's mother sells her husband's old shoes for money for Salim.

Event 4:
Salim uses the money to buy a dog.

▶ Try This

Events Chart Jigsaw

Make an events chart like the one on the facing page showing how one thing leads to another in the story.

1. Work in groups of four. Write down each event that happens in the story. Number each event and write each one on a separate card as shown on the facing page.
2. Arrange the cards on a sheet of paper in the order that the events happened. Look for events that caused other events to happen. Draw arrows between these events. The example on the facing page will get you started.
3. Retell the story to the class using the events chart that you made as a guide.

▶ Learning About Literature

Plot Profile

The plot of a story is what happens. In every plot there are "highs" (more exciting events) and "lows" (less exciting events). Rising action leads to a high point and falling action leads to a low point. A plot profile gives you an idea of the highs and lows in "The Carpenter's Son."

1. List twelve important events from the story. (See the illustration below.)
2. Decide how exciting each event is, and put a dot in a numbered row on the Plot Profile. The higher the number, the more exciting the event.
3. Connect the dots to get a picture of when the highs and lows of the plot happen.

List of Events	Plot Profile											
1. *Salim buys a cat.*	10											
2. *Salim buys a dog.*	9											
3.	8											
4.	7											
5.	6											
6.	5											
7.	4											
8.	3											
9.	2											
10.	1											
11.												
12.	Event	1	2	3	4	5	6	7	8	9	10	11	12

(Vertical axis label: Level of Excitement)

▶ Exploring Your Own Experience

Sharing Your Ideas

1. First, think for a few minutes about what the dream of freedom means to you.
2. Next, tell a partner what your thoughts were.
3. Finally, with your partner, join another pair of partners. Take turns talking, each person telling the group what his or her partner's thoughts were.

▶ Background

In the United States during the 1950s and 1960s, several groups organized to fight for the rights of African Americans. They wanted to change segregation laws (rules that kept blacks and whites apart) and laws that made it difficult for minorities to vote. Through the leadership of Martin Luther King, Jr. and other leaders, as well as the efforts of thousands of people, many changes occurred.

People tried to change opinions by holding marches and rallies (when many people get together to show support for an idea). Martin Luther King, Jr. made a famous speech at a national rally on August 28, 1963, at the Lincoln Memorial in Washington, D.C. Over 250,000 people came that day. Some parts of this important speech are included in the following abridged version.

I Have a Dream

by

Martin Luther King, Jr.

I HAVE A DREAM. IT IS A DREAM DEEPLY ROOTED IN THE American Dream. I have a dream that one day this nation will rise up and live out the true meaning of its creed: "We hold these truths to be self-evident, that all men are created equal."

I have a dream that one day on the red hills of Georgia sons of former slaves and sons of former slaveowners will be able to sit down together at the table of brotherhood.

I have a dream that one day my four little children will live in a nation where they will not be judged by the color of their skin but by the content of their character.

I have a dream that one day every valley shall be exalted, every hill and mountain shall be made low. The rough places will be made plain, and the crooked places will be made straight. This is the faith that I go back to the South with. With this faith we shall be able to hew out of the mountain of despair a stone of hope. With this faith we will be able to

creed belief

be self-evident speak for themselves; obvious, easily understood

exalted heightened, raised

faith belief

hew carve, cut

despair deep sadness, loss of hope

Welders by Ben Shahn, 1944

work together, to pray together, to struggle together, to go to jail together, to stand up for freedom, knowing we will be free one day.

This will be the day when all of God's children will be able to sing with new meaning, "Let freedom ring." So let freedom ring from the prodigious hilltops of New Hampshire. Let freedom ring from the mighty mountains of New York. But not only that. Let freedom ring from Stone Mountain of Georgia. Let freedom ring from every molehill of

---

ring sound, fill the air
prodigious wonderful, amazing, very large
molehill small pile of dirt

Mississippi, from every mountainside.

When we allow freedom to ring—when we let it ring from every village and every hamlet, from every state and every city, we will be able to speed up that day when all of God's children, black men and white men, Jews and Gentiles, Protestants and Catholics, will be able to join hands and sing in the words of the old Negro spiritual, "Free at last! Free at last! Thank God Almighty, we are free at last!"

....

hamlet   very small village or town

ABOUT THE AUTHOR

Martin Luther King, Jr., a Baptist minister and the son of a Baptist minister, received the Nobel Peace Prize in 1964 for his work for peoples' rights in the United States.

King was a minister in Montgomery, Alabama, when he led the Montgomery bus boycott. When Mrs. Rosa Parks refused to give up her seat in the bus to a white man, as required by city law, people in Montgomery demanded a change by refusing to ride the buses. The boycott lasted for more than a year.

King continued his work until he was killed on April 4, 1968, in Memphis, Tennessee, where he was organizing protest demonstrations for the rights of poor workers.

Martin Luther King, Jr.'s birthday is observed as a federal holiday in the United States.

▶ **Martin Luther King, Jr. (1929–1968)** ◀

▶ *What Do You Think?*

Think about Dr. King's speech and discuss your ideas with your classmates and teacher. Here are some other ideas and questions to think and talk about:

1. What do you think Dr. King means by "the American Dream"?
2. What was Dr. King's dream in 1963 for his children? Do you think it has come true?
3. What does Dr. King think the world will be like when people are "free at last"?
4. How does this idea compare to ideas about freedom you discussed before reading the speech?
5. Does Dr. King repeat anything in his speech? What words? How many times? What effect does this have on people hearing the speech?

▶ *Learning About Literature*

How Do You Write a Speech?

A speech is meant to be spoken. Great speakers use simple language to make clear points and evoke powerful images. Here are some characteristics of good speeches:

- Sentences are shorter than sentences meant to be read.
- Organization is clear and straightforward.
- Memorable words or ideas are repeated.
- Strong, colorful words are used.

Look back over Dr. King's speech and find examples of these characteristics. If possible, watch a video or listen to a recording of Dr. King giving this speech. How does his delivery add to the power of the words? Use a chart like this to help you.

Speech Example Chart

Characteristic	Example from Dr. King's Speech
1. Short sentences	
2. Clear organization	
3. Memorable key phrases	
4. Strong, colorful words	
5. Other	

▶ Try This

Draft a Speech

Use Dr. King's speech as a model to write your own speech. Choose a topic that is important to you such as world peace, protecting the environment, or avoiding drugs. Use Dr. King's "I have a dream" to begin each new section of your speech, or think up a phrase of your own such as "My hope for the world is."

Suggestions:

1. Start each paragraph with your repeated phrase.
2. Give examples to show what your hope or dream is.
3. Try to write three or more paragraphs.
4. Keep your sentences short and clear.

▶ Writing

Conferring and Responding to Writing AM

Working in groups of four or five members, each person reads his or her draft. Then, group members respond to the writer.

- Encourage the writer by pointing out strengths (good parts) of the speech.
- Ask questions about things that you want to know more about.
- Make suggestions on how to make the speech stronger. (Refer to the chart on the facing page.)

Each group member makes a chart with the following information for each speech.

1. Strengths
2. Questions
3. Good speech characteristics:

   - examples of short sentences
   - examples showing clear organization
   - some memorable key phrases
   - some strong, colorful words

4. Suggestions

▶ *Exploring Your Own Experience*

Paper Folding

The paper crane pictured below is an example of the Japanese art of origami, or paper folding. Show your classmates how to make any other folded paper figures you know of and tell any stories that go with them.

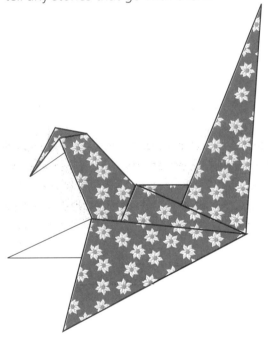

▶ *Background*

Sadako and the Thousand Paper Cranes is based on the life of a real little girl who lived in Japan from 1943 to 1955.

She was in Hiroshima when the United States Air Force dropped an atom bomb on that city in an attempt to end World War II. Ten years later she died as a result of radiation from the bomb.

Her courage made Sadako a heroine to children in Japan. This is the story of Sadako.

The Golden Crane

from
Sadako and the Thousand Paper Cranes
by Eleanor Coerr

THE NEXT MORNING SADAKO WOKE up slowly. She listened for the familiar sounds of her mother making breakfast, but there were only the new and different sounds of a hospital. Sadako sighed. She had hoped that yesterday was just a bad dream. It was even more real when Nurse Yasunaga came in to give her a shot.

"Getting shots is part of being in the hospital," the plump nurse said briskly. "You'll get used to it."

"I just want the sickness to be over with," Sadako said unhappily, "so I can go home."

That afternoon Chizuko was Sadako's first visitor. She smiled mysteriously as she held something behind her back. "Shut your eyes," she said. While Sadako squinted her eyes tightly shut, Chizuko put some pieces of paper and scissors on the bed, "Now you can look," she said.

"What is it?" Sadako asked, staring at the paper.

Chizuko was pleased with herself. "I've figured out a way for you to get well," she said proudly. "Watch!" She cut a piece of gold paper into a large square. In a short time she had folded it over and over into a beautiful crane.

Sadako was puzzled. "But how can that paper bird make me well?"

"Don't you remember that old story about the crane?" Chizuko asked. "It's supposed to live for a thousand years. If a sick person folds one thousand paper cranes, the gods will grant her wish and make her healthy again." She handed the crane to Sadako. "Here's your first one."

Sadako's eyes filled with tears. How

---

give her a shot give medicine with a needle
to be over with to end, to be finished

figured out discovered, found out

Memory of Sandhill Cranes by Roger Brown, 1981

kind of Chizuko to bring a good luck charm! Especially when her friend didn't really believe in such things. Sadako took the golden crane and made a wish. The funniest little feeling came over her when she touched the bird. It must be a good omen.

"Thank you, Chizuko chan," she whispered. "I'll never part with it."

WHEN SHE BEGAN TO WORK WITH the paper, Sadako discovered that folding a crane wasn't as easy as it looked. With Chizuko's help she learned how to do the difficult parts. After making ten birds, Sadako lined them up on the table beside the golden crane. Some were a bit lopsided, but it was a beginning.

---

good luck charm object to bring good luck
omen sign
chan Japanese word that is used with names to show familiarity or fondness, like Pep*ito* in Spanish or Mik*ey* in English

lopsided crooked, bent over

"Now I have only nine hundred and ninety to make," Sadako said. With the golden crane nearby she felt safe and lucky. Why, in a few weeks she would be able to finish the thousand. Then she would be strong enough to go home.

That evening Masahiro brought Sadako's homework from school. When he saw the cranes, he said, "There isn't enough room on that small table to show off your birds. I'll hang them from the ceiling for you."

Sadako was smiling all over. "Do you promise to hang every crane I make?" she asked.

Masahiro promised.
"That's fine!" Sadako said, her eyes twinkling with mischief. "Then you'll hang the whole thousand?"

"A thousand!" Her brother groaned. "You're joking!"

Sadako told him the story of the cranes.

Masahiro ran a hand through his straight black hair. "You tricked me!" he said with a grin. "But I'll do it anyhow." He borrowed some thread and tacks from Nurse Yasunaga and hung the first ten cranes. The golden crane stayed in its place of honor on the table.

AFTER SUPPER MRS. SASAKI BROUGHT Mitsue and Eiji to the hospital. Everyone was surprised to see the birds. They reminded Mrs. Sasaki of a famous old poem.

> Out of colored paper, cranes
> come flying into
> our house.

Mitsue and Eiji liked the golden crane best. But Mrs. Sasaki chose the tiniest one made of fancy green paper with pink parasols on it. "This is my choice," she said, "because small ones are the most difficult to make."

After visiting hours it was lonely in the hospital room. So lonely that Sadako folded more cranes to keep up her courage.

> Eleven . . . I wish I'd get better.
> Twelve . . . I wish I'd get better.

---

twinkling shining, sparkling
mischief naughty fun

tiniest very smallest
parasols umbrellas used as shades

Color Streamers Hang in Memorial Park for Hiroshima Victims by P. J. Griffiths/Magnum, 1981

Epilogue

Sadako Sasaki died on October 25, 1955.

Her classmates folded three hundred and fifty-six cranes so that one thousand were buried with Sadako. In a way she got her wish. She will live on in the hearts of people for a long time.

After the funeral the bamboo class collected Sadako's letters and published them in a book. They called it *Kokeshi*, after the doll they had given to Sadako while she was in the hospital. The book was sent around Japan and soon everyone knew about Sadako and her thousand paper cranes.

Sadako's friends began to dream of building a monument to her and all children killed by the atom bomb. Young people throughout the country helped collect money for the project. Finally their dream came true. In 1958 the statue was unveiled in the Hiroshima Peace Park. There is Sadako, standing on top of a granite mountain of paradise. She is holding a golden crane in outstretched hands.

A Folded Crane Club was organized in her honor. Members still place thousands of paper cranes beneath Sadako's statue on August 6— Peace Day. They make a wish, too. Their wish is engraved on the base of the statue:

This is our cry,
this is our prayer;
peace in the world.

---

unveiled uncovered, shown

paradise heaven

outstretched extended, opened, reaching

ABOUT THE AUTHOR

Eleanor Coerr was born in 1922 in Saskatchewan, Canada. She has traveled widely as a writer, editor, and wife of a career diplomat. Her books for young people have been set in Japan, Thailand, and Taiwan. Coerr worked to establish and promote the first children's library in Ecuador.

▶ **Eleanor Coerr (born 1922)** ◀

▶ *What Do You Think?*

Think about the story and discuss your ideas with your classmates and teacher. Here are other ideas and questions to think and talk about. Use examples from the story to support your ideas.

1. What was Sadako's dream?
2. What led Sadako to try to make 1,000 paper cranes?
3. Why is Sadako important to the children of Japan? What was special about her?
4. How did Sadako's life cause a monument to be built to victims of atomic bombs dropped on Hiroshima and Nagasaki?
5. Nonfiction may be written to inform, to persuade, to express an opinion, or to entertain. What do you think was Eleanor Coerr's purpose for writing this story?

▶ *Learning About Literature*

Character Development

Each person in a story is called a character. The main character is the most important person in a story. Sadako is the main character in "The Golden Crane." The other characters are minor characters. Chizuko, Sadako's friend, and Masahiro, Sadako's brother, are minor characters.

Writers bring characters to life in several ways. They use a character's words or actions to tell about a character, they describe the character, and they describe a character by what other people in the story say about the character.

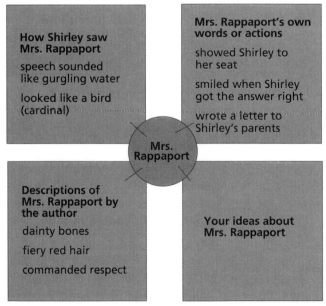

How Shirley saw Mrs. Rappaport

speech sounded like gurgling water

looked like a bird (cardinal)

Mrs. Rappaport's own words or actions

showed Shirley to her seat

smiled when Shirley got the answer right

wrote a letter to Shirley's parents

Mrs. Rappaport

Descriptions of Mrs. Rappaport by the author

dainty bones

fiery red hair

commanded respect

Your ideas about Mrs. Rappaport

▶ *Try This*

Character Web

A character web helps you to outline important ideas about a character.

1 Look at the sample character web on the facing page. It describes Mrs. Rappaport, the teacher in "China's Little Ambassador."

2. Make a character web for Sadako. Put her name in the center of your web.

3. Write words around Sadako's name that describe her. Use:
   - Sadako's own words or actions
   - descriptions of Sadako by the author
   - what others say to or about Sadako
   - your own ideas about Sadako

Draw lines from your descriptions to the name *Sadako*.

4. Now, identify similar characteristics from your descriptive words. Make a second web with similar words grouped together.

▶ *Writing*

Character Sketch

Use your character web to write a one- or two- paragraph character sketch of Sadako. Illustrate it with a pencil or ink sketch of Sadako.

Editing Checklist

Use the editing checklist below to check your paper for common errors. Make needed corrections. When you have finished your character sketches, share them with one another, and then post them on a bulletin board or bind them into a class book.

- Do all sentences begin with a capital letter?
- Do all sentences end with a punctuation mark? (. ! or ?)
- Did you indent the beginning of each paragraph?
- Do all sentences have a subject and a verb?
- Did you look up any words that might be misspelled?

Unit Follow-Up

▶ Making Connections

Unit Project Ideas

Here are some possible unit projects. If you want, think up a project of your own. You can use some of the techniques you learned in this unit (appealing to the senses, plot profiles, character sketches, and character webs) to help you plan and complete your project.

1. A Mini-Speech Contest. Hold a speech contest in which each class member gives a five-minute speech on the theme of the unit: Wishes and Dreams. Each audience member can give feedback to the speaker.

2. Biography of a Dreamer. Make a character web of someone from the unit who interests you. Use the ideas on the web to write a short biography of the character. The author biographies in this book may serve as models.

3. Dream Journal. Use a journal to write down your dreams every day for two weeks. You may include your dreams while sleeping as well as your wishes, hopes, and dreams while awake. At the end of two weeks, reread your journal to see whether it contains any ideas you want to develop further and rewrite for sharing or for publication.

4. Your Autobiography.
- On a long strip of adding machine tape (or strips of paper taped together), list all of the years since your birth. Leave about a foot after each year.
- After each year, write important events that took place in your life that year. This is a time line of your life.
- Plot important events on a plot profile.
- Write an autobiography using the information on the time line and plot profile. Select the events you rated most exciting on your plot profile.
- Share your autobiography with classmates, friends, and family. Keep it in a safe place for future reference.

5. Your Future Biography. Make an event chart or time line of your goals for the future and how you will get there. Use a plot profile to predict the highlights of your future.

Further Reading

Here are some books related to this unit that you might enjoy.

- *A Jar of Dreams,* by Yoshiko Uchida. Macmillan, 1981. A family's dreams help them overcome the difficulties of being Japanese Americans in Depression-era (1930s) California.

- *Folk Tales from Asia for Children Everywhere,* 6 volumes, Asian Cultural Center for UNESCO. John Weatherhill, Inc., 1975–1977. This illustrated collection includes "The Carpenter's Son."

- *Langston Hughes, American Poet,* by Alice Walker. Thomas Y. Crowell, 1974. The famous writer tells about Hughes's difficult and fascinating life.

- *The Life and Words of Martin Luther King,* by Ira Peck. Scholastic, 1986. Includes biographical information, photographs, and selected writings and speeches.

- *Lupita Mañana,* by Patricia Beatty. William Morrow, 1981. Two teenagers, brother and sister, must leave their rural Mexican home and cross the border illegally to find work in the United States.

- *Sadako and the Thousand Paper Cranes,* by Eleanor Coerr. G. P. Putnam's Sons, 1977. The complete story of Sadako.

- *Selected Poems of Langston Hughes,* by Langston Hughes. Random, 1959, 1990. The author's own choices.

- *The Witch of Fourth Street and Other Stories,* by Myron Levoy. Harper & Row, 1974. A collection of short stories about the lives and dreams of immigrant families in New York City in the early 1900s.

Christmas at Home by Grandma Moses, 1946

Generations

This last unit focuses on the relationships between people of different ages. Through two poems, two stories, and a play, you can look at how family members from different generations love, teach, and learn from one another.

▶ *Exploring Your Own Experience*

Then and Now

Many things have changed about family life in modern times—we have televisions and VCRs while our grandparents had only newspapers, books, and stories. Yet some things stay the same about families, no matter how the times change.

All families have their own activities and ways of doing things, such as sharing family meals and free time. To help you think about activities in your family, make a three-column chart like the one below.

- In the first column, list things that your family used to do five, ten, and twenty or more years ago.
- In the second column, list things that your family does today.
- In the third column, write whether the things have changed or stayed the same. Discuss your charts with your classmates and teacher.

▶ *Background*

Leroy Quintana's poem explores both things that change and things that stay the same in family life. You will notice there are no capital letters in this poem. Poets sometimes do this for understatement, visual appeal, or to give all the words equal importance.

Things My Family Did Years Ago	*Things My Family Does Today*	*Changed or Stayed the Same?*
1.	1.	
2.	2.	

Piñones

by
Leroy Quintana

when i was young
we would sit by
an old firewood stove
watching my grandmother make candy,
listening to the stories
my grandparents would tell
about "the old days"
                              and eat piñones

---

piñones pine nuts

Mural Detail, Tucson, AZ by John Cancalosi, photo, c. 1990

now we belong
to a supersonic age
and have college degrees.
we sit around color t.v. sets
watching the super bowl
listening to howard cosell,
stories of rioting, war, inflation
and eat piñones

---

supersonic faster than sound
howard cosell well-known U.S. TV sports
announcer of the 1960s and 1970s
rioting when many people are in a fight, often
with property damaged and people hurt
inflation rising prices; when the same amount
of money buys less than in the past

ABOUT THE AUTHOR

Leroy Quintana grew up in New Mexico, always fascinated by the *cuentos* (stories) of the older people he knew. His writing draws from the rich oral tradition of his Mexican roots. In addition to being a writer, Quintana has worked as a roofer, a soldier in Vietnam, and a counselor.

▶ **Leroy Quintana** ◀

▶ *What Do You Think?*

Think about the poem and discuss your ideas with your classmates and teacher. Here are some questions to talk about.

1. What is the cultural background of the family in the poem? What makes you think this?
2. What did the family do in the old days? Are any of these activities on your chart?
3. What does the family do now? Are any of these activities on your chart?
4. How has the family changed and how has the family stayed the same?
5. Although Quintana mentions activities that families do together, poems can often be understood on more than one level. What does the author say about family life in general with this poem? How have modern families changed? How has life become more complicated?
6. Can you tell how the poet feels about the "supersonic age"? Do you think the poet is happy or sad about the things that have changed? Do you agree with him?
7. Notice how Quintana does not use capital letters in his poem. In addition, he uses very little punctuation. How do you know how to read the poem aloud?

▶ *Try This*

Lists of Memories

Your memory is one of the most important tools for becoming a powerful writer. Since you were a child, ideas have been collecting in your head about many things such as learning to ride a bike, falling off, arriving and leaving, and the way the air smelled on a certain summer day. These are all sources for your writing.

A list is a simple way to put your memories in writing. First, make a list of possible topics you want to explore. Your family is probably one of your richest sources of memories. Then choose a topic and make a list of words and ideas about that topic. Share your list with a friend, then add more ideas that sharing reminded you of.

▶ *Learning About Literature*

Breaking Rules

Learning and following the rules of capitalization and punctuation are essential writing skills. Yet poets like Quintana break these rules, choosing to use no capitalization or punctuation or making up their own new rules. Poetry is an outlet for playfulness and creativity with language that sometimes means new rules.

With a partner, discuss "breaking rules" in writing.

- What are Quintana's new rules?
- Why do you think he uses these rules? Do you think they make his poem better?

Now choose a paragraph—something from you or your partner's writing, or a paragraph from the school newspaper, for example. Rewrite the paragraph using new rules that you and your partner have decided upon. Share it with the class and give reasons for your new rules.

▶ *Writing*

Use ideas from your "then and now" charts and from your list of memories to develop a short poem about your past. In a second draft, experiment with breaking rules of capitalization, punctuation, and the use of space on a page. Share them with a small group of classmates. Do your new rules work? Which draft do you like better? Consider polishing for publication a third draft with the best elements of the first two.

▶ *Exploring Your Own Experience*

Show, Don't Tell—A Guessing Game

Describe someone in your class using only the person's actual words and actions. Write on a sheet of paper some things the person often says or does. Then read your paper aloud and see whether the other students can guess who it is. Be sure not to describe what the person looks like. Use only the person's actual words or actions.

▶ *Background*

William Carlos Williams writes poetry about everyday life in simple, everyday language. He chooses his words very carefully and often arranges them in short lines to show the importance of each detail. In this poem he writes about the death of his grandmother.

The Last Words of My English Grandmother

by
William Carlos Williams

There were some dirty plates
and a glass of milk
beside her on a small table
near the rank, disheveled bed—

Wrinkled and nearly blind
she lay and snored
rousing with anger in her tones
to cry for food,

---

rank bad-smelling
disheveled messy
rousing waking up

Gimme something to eat—
They're starving me—
I'm all right I won't go
to the hospital. No, no, no.

Give me something to eat
Let me take you
to the hospital, I said
and after you are well

you can do as you please.
She smiled, Yes
you do what you please first
then I can do what I please—

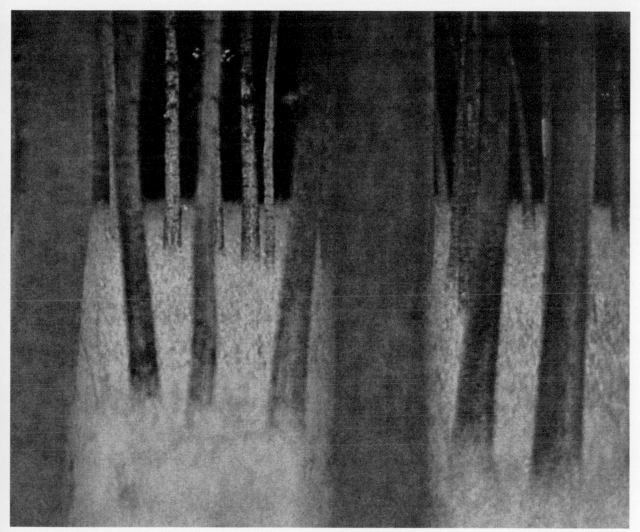

Compiegne (detail) by Andre Martin, c. 1965

Oh, oh, oh! she cried
as the ambulance men lifted
her to the stretcher—
Is this what you call

making me comfortable?
By now her mind was clear—
Oh you think you're smart
you young people,

she said, but I'll tell you
you don't know anything.
Then we started.
On the way
we passed a long row
of elms. She looked at them
awhile out of
the ambulance window and said,

What are all those
fuzzy-looking things out there?
Trees? Well, I'm tired
of them and rolled her head away.

William Carlos Williams, son of an English father and a Puerto Rican mother, was a medical doctor as well as a writer of poetry, novels, and plays. His writing reflects the life experiences and everyday language of the people he knew.

▶ **William Carlos Williams (1883–1963)** ◀

▶ *What Do You Think?*

Think about the poem and discuss your ideas with your classmates and teacher. Here are some questions to talk about.

1. In the *Show, Don't Tell* activity before the poem, you practiced using someone's words and actions to describe that person. Find examples of the grandmother's words and actions in the poem. What do they tell you about her?

2. Imagine you are the grandmother. How do you feel about dying?

3. Imagine you are the grandson. How do you feel about watching your grandmother die?

4. William Carlos Williams doesn't use quotation marks to tell when the grandmother is speaking. Do you think he should? Why?

5. The grandmother says about young people:

   > Oh you think you're smart
   > you young people,
   >
   > she said, but I'll tell you
   > you don't know anything.

   a. What do you think she is thinking about?

   b. Do you know other older people who say this about young people? What do you think they are thinking about?

   c. What do young people know best? What do old people know best?

   d. What are some things that young people don't understand very well?

▶ *Try This*

From Poetry to Narrative

Working alone or with a partner, choose a stanza from either of the two poems. Copy it in your notebook. Rewrite it as a prose narrative, or story, telling what you think is happening in that stanza. You don't have to limit yourself to what the poet wrote. You can add your interpretation (your ideas and thoughts), which will be different from everyone else's. When you are finished, show your interpretation to a partner. For example, below is an example using the first stanza of the William Carlos Williams poem.

> There were some dirty plates
> and a glass of milk
> beside her on a small table
> near the rank, disheveled bed—

Now read one person's narrative interpretation:

> He hadn't heard from his grandmother for a long time, so he went to see her. She was very sick—too sick to take care of her house or herself, but she was too stubborn to ask for help.

While the poet shows objects in the room, he doesn't tell what they mean. The narrative interpretation explains what one reader thinks the objects mean. Someone else might have a different opinion. Note also that the narrative added details ("he hadn't heard from his grandmother") to make it more interesting.

▶ Learning About Literature

How do Poets Show and Not Tell?

In Unit 1 we discussed how poetry differs from prose in the way words are arranged on the page. Poetry also differs from prose because it uses fewer words to say something. Each word in poetry, therefore, has more importance. Poets choose their words carefully, often leaving much of the thinking to the reader. Poets begin a conversation; readers must complete it.

1. Count the words in the stanza you chose. Then count the words in your narrative interpretation of that stanza. Was your narrative interpretation longer than the stanza you rewrote? Why does prose usually use more words than poetry?
2. Review other poems in this book. Do they present more information than prose usually does with the same number of words? Do the poems show actions, rather than tell about them? Give examples from the poems to support your answers.

▶ Writing

A Place

Write a poem about a place you like very much. Keep your writing simple, and use specific details. You might want to go back to the exercise about appealing to the reader's senses of sight, hearing, smell, taste, and touch (page 130). You can present details and thoughts that show your feelings, which the readers must interpret. Use short lines. Think of a good title—perhaps the name of the place. Share your poem with your classmates. Try interpreting one another's poems.

▶ *Exploring Your Own Experience*

A Memory

Think of a very important event in your life. It might be a birth, a death, a marriage, an accident, or an important achievement. Try to picture the event in your mind. Write down a brief description of what you see. Try to include particulars. Some people may like to share descriptions with classmates.

▶ *Background*

Although this selection is from a fiction book, it is written as a personal memory, or *memoir.* A young child remembers when she found out about her grandfather's death from her father.

Papa Who Wakes Up Tired in the Dark

by

Sandra Cisneros

YOUR ABUELITO IS DEAD, PAPA SAYS EARLY one morning in my room. *Está muerto*, and then as if he just heard the news himself, crumples like a coat and cries, my brave Papa cries. I have never seen my Papa cry and don't know what to do.

I know he will have to go away, that he will take a plane to Mexico, all the uncles and aunts will be there, and they will have a black and white photo taken in front of the tomb with flowers shaped like spears in a white vase because this is how they send the dead away in that country.

----

abuelito grandfather
Está muerto He is dead
crumples wrinkles into a ball
tomb grave, burial place

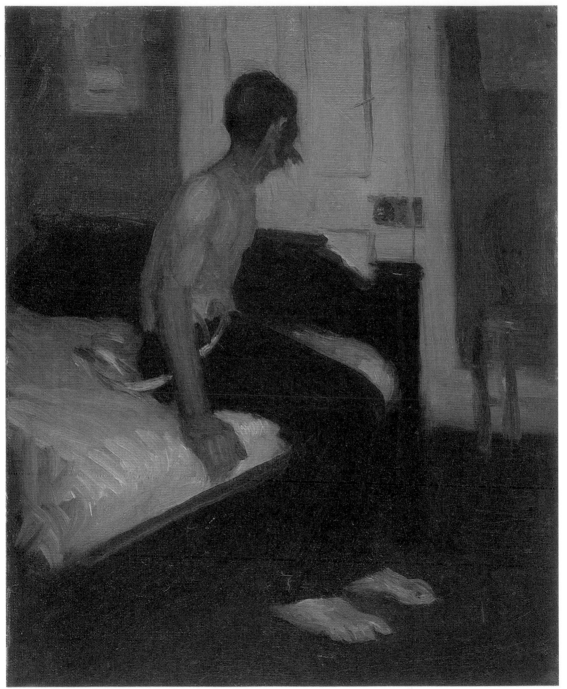

Man Seated on Bed by Edward Hopper, c. 1905–6

Because I am the oldest, my father has told me first, and now it is my turn to tell the others. I will have to explain why we can't play. I will have to tell them to be quiet today.

My Papa, his thick hands and thick shoes, who wakes up tired in the dark, who combs his hair with water, drinks his coffee, and is gone before we wake, today is sitting on my bed.

And I think if my own Papa died what would I do. I hold my Papa in my arms. I hold and hold and hold him.

ABOUT THE AUTHOR

Sandra Cisneros, who resides in California, is the daughter of a Mexican father and a Mexican-American mother. She wants to tell stories about people whose lives are seldom written about. She feels lucky to know two languages because she has twice as many words to choose from as other writers have.

▶ **Sandra Cisneros (born 1954)** ◀

▶ *What Do You Think?*

Think about the story and discuss your ideas with your classmates and teacher. Here are some questions to talk about.

1. Prose, too, can show and not tell. What do you learn about the family from the details, or specific facts, in this short piece?

2. Can you find examples of poetic devices such as metaphors and similes?

3. What would change if Cisneros arranged this selection in short lines like Williams's poem? Use the following example:

> Your abuelito
> is dead, Papa says
> early one morning
> in my room.
>
> *Está muerto,* and then
> as if he just heard the news
> himself,
> crumples like a coat and
> cries,
> my brave Papa
> cries.

Do you read the story differently when it is set up like a poem? How? What are some differences between prose and poetry?

▶ *Try This*

Venn Diagram

Use a Venn diagram to compare and contrast William Carlos Williams's and Sandra Cisneros's selections about the death of a grandparent. Consider such aspects as:

- the genre, or type of writing
- who is telling about the event

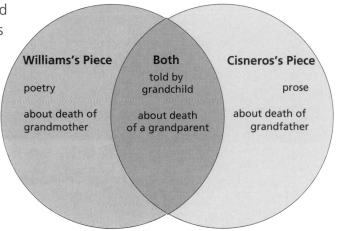

Williams's Piece

poetry

about death of grandmother

Both

told by grandchild

about death of a grandparent

Cisneros's Piece

prose

about death of grandfather

▶ Learning About Literature

Memoirs and Journals

Many writers keep journals in which they write down their thoughts and what happens to them. As well as providing writing practice, these journals often provide material for later works that may be published. Memoirs have value for individuals who want to remember their lives, for those who love literature, and for historians and social scientists as well. Discuss the following:

1. Have you ever kept a diary or journal?
2. Do you know anyone who has? Why did they do it?
3. What important things have happened to you this year that you would like to remember?
4. What are some good reasons to keep a journal?

▶ Writing

Journal-Keeping

If you don't already have a journal, start one. Buy an inexpensive notebook. Plan time to write in your journal several times each week. Read your journal occasionally. It will be a good source of topics to develop further when you write.

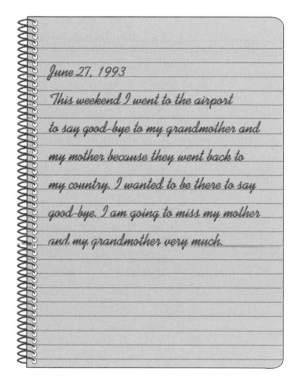

June 27, 1993

This weekend I went to the airport to say good-bye to my grandmother and my mother because they went back to my country. I wanted to be there to say good-bye. I am going to miss my mother and my grandmother very much.

▶ *Exploring Your Own Experience*

The Statue of Liberty

Look at the picture of the Statue of Liberty on page 186. With your class, list words that the statue makes you think of. Try to group the words into categories and then write them on a chart as a cluster diagram. (See p. 48.) Discuss the different responses that people have to this symbolic statue.

For millions of immigrants, the Statue of Liberty symbolizes the promise of freedom and opportunity. This ideal is powerfully expressed in Emma Lazarus's famous poem entitled "The New Colossus," which is inscribed on a bronze plaque placed on the pedestal of the monument. The poem ends with these lines:

NOT LIKE THE BRAZEN GIANT OF GREEK FAME,
WITH CONQUERING LIMBS ASTRIDE FROM LAND TO LAND;
HERE AT OUR SEA-WASHED, SUNSET GATES SHALL STAND
A MIGHTY WOMAN WITH A TORCH, WHOSE FLAME
IS THE IMPRISONED LIGHTNING, AND HER NAME
MOTHER OF EXILES. FROM HER BEACON-HAND
GLOWS WORLD-WIDE WELCOME; HER EYES COMMAND
THE AIR-BRIDGED HARBOR THAT TWIN CITIES FRAME.
"KEEP, ANCIENT LANDS, YOUR STORIED POMP!" CRIES SHE
WITH SILENT LIPS. "GIVE ME YOUR TIRED, YOUR POOR,
YOUR HUDDLED MASSES YEARNING TO BREATHE FREE,
THE WRETCHED REFUSE OF YOUR TEEMING SHORE.
SEND THESE, THE HOMELESS, TEMPEST-TOST TO ME.
I LIFT MY LAMP BESIDE THE GOLDEN DOOR!"

▶ *Background*

The Statue of Liberty stands in New York Harbor to welcome all who enter. It was a gift to the United States from France in 1884. It had no pedestal, or support, to stand on, so the people of the United States, many of them immigrants, collected the money for it.

Grandpa and the Statue is an adapted version of a play written for radio about these events. The playwright uses only voices and sound effects to create the scene and mood for the play.

Grandpa and the Statue

by

Arthur Miller

CHARACTERS (In order of appearance)

Young Monaghan (Child Monaghan grown up)
Grandfather Monaghan
Child Monaghan
Alf
Girl
Young Man
Megaphone Voice
Veteran

This is the story of a young boy and his immigrant grandfather, and their first visit to the Statue of Liberty. Grandfather Monaghan was the stingiest man in Brooklyn, New York. The neighbors called him "Mercyless" Monaghan. He even used to save umbrella handles just because he couldn't stand seeing anything go to waste.

In 1887, Grandpa Monaghan lived on Butler Street. One day he was sitting on the front porch, reading a paper he borrowed from the neighbors, when Jack Sheean from up the street stopped by. Jack wanted "Mercyless" Monaghan to contribute to the Statue of Liberty fund. It seems that the French sent the statue over, but there was no stand to put it on. Immigrants from all over the country were reaching into their pockets and putting in for a base for the statue to stand on. Everyone on Butler Street had given

---

stingiest most unwilling to spend money, cheapest

putting in giving money

Horse Drinking Fountain, Fulton Street at Lafayette Avenue, c. 1893

money—everyone except Grandpa Monaghan. At first he told Jack Sheean that he wouldn't contribute to something he hadn't seen. When Jack took him to the warehouse to see it, still in pieces, Grandpa Monaghan concocted a story that the statue would fall down in the first wind because it was hollow.

In fact, Grandpa Monaghan even convinced his grandson that the statue would fall in the first big wind. And he, in turn, convinced his friends. But as the seasons came and went, and the winds blew and died out, the statue was still said to remain standing. Finally, one day, Young Monaghan got up the nerve to ask his old grandpa if they could take the ferry to go and see the great statue.

....

concocted made up
hollow empty inside

[*Music up and down*]
[*Creaking of a rocking chair*]
Grandfather Monaghan: Huh?
Child Monaghan: Can you stop rocking for a minute?
[*Rocking stops*]
Can you put down your paper?
[*Rustle of paper*]
I—I read the weather report for tomorrow.
Grandfather Monaghan: The weather report . . .
Child Monaghan: Yeh. It says fair and cool.
Grandfather Monaghan: What of it?
Child Monaghan: I was wondering. Supposing you and me we went on a boat tomorrow. You know, I see the water every day when I go down to the docks to play, but I never sat on it. I mean in a boat.
Grandfather Monaghan: Oh. Well, we might take the ferry on the Jersey side. We might do that.
Child Monaghan: Yeh, but there's nothing to see in Jersey.
Grandfather Monaghan: You can't go to Europe tomorrow.
Child Monaghan: No, but couldn't we go toward the ocean? Just . . . toward it?
Grandfather Monaghan: Toward it.

What—what is it on your mind, boy? What is it now?
Child Monaghan: Well, I . . .
Grandfather Monaghan: Oh, you want to take the Staten Island ferry. Sure, that's in the direction of the sea.
Child Monaghan: No, grampa, not the Staten Island ferry.
Grandfather Monaghan: You don't mean—[*Breaks off*] Boy!
Child Monaghan: All the kids are going tomorrow with Georgie's old man.
Grandfather Monaghan: You don't believe me any more.
Child Monaghan: I do, grampa, but . . .
Grandfather Monaghan: You don't. If you did you'd stay clear of the Statue of Liberty for love of your life.
Child Monaghan: But, grampa, when is it going to fall down? All I do is wait and wait.
Grandfather Monaghan: [*With some uncertainty*] You've got to have faith.
Child Monaghan: But every kid in my class went to see it and now the ones that didn't are going tomorrow. And they all keep talking about it and all I do . . . Well, I can't keep telling them it's a swindle. I—I wish we could see it, grampa. It don't cost so much to go.

stay clear of avoid, stay away from
swindle trick to get someone's money

Grandpa and the Statue **183**

Grandfather Monaghan: As long as you put it that way I'll have to admit I'm a bit curious meself as to how it's managed to stand upright so long. Tell you what I'll do. Barrin' wind, we'll chance it tomorrow.

Child Monaghan: Oh, gramp!

Grandfather Monaghan: But! If anyone should ask you where we went you'll say—Staten Island. Are y' on?

Child Monaghan: Okay, sure. Staten Island.

Grandfather Monaghan: [*Secretively*] We'll take the early boat, then. Mum's the word, now. For if old man Sheean hears that I went out there I'll have no peace from the thief the rest of m' life. [*Music up and down*]

[*Boat whistles*]

Child Monaghan: Gee, it's nice ridin' on a boat, ain't it, grampa?

Grandfather Monaghan: Never said there was anything wrong with the boat. Boat's all right. You're sure now that Georgie's father is takin' the kids in the afternoon.

Child Monaghan: Yeh, that's when they're going. Gee, look at those two sea gulls. Wee!—look at them swoop! They caught a fish!

Grandfather Monaghan: What I can't understand is what all these people see in that statue that they'll keep a boat like this full makin' the trip, year in year out. To hear the newspapers talk, if the statue was gone we'd be at war with the nation that stole her the followin' mornin' early. All it is is a big high pile of French copper.

Child Monaghan: The teachers says it shows us that we got liberty.

Grandfather Monaghan: Bah! If you've got liberty you don't need a statue to tell you you got it; and if you haven't got liberty no statue's going to do you any good tellin' you you got it. It was a criminal waste of the people's money. [*Quietly*] And just to prove it to you I'll ask this feller sitting right over there what he sees in it. You'll see what a madness the whole thing was. Say, mister?

Alf: Hey?

Grandfather Monaghan: I beg your pardon. I'm a little strange here, and curious. Could you tell me why you're

---

put it say it
meself myself
barrin' unless there is
are y'on? Okay? Do you agree
mum's the word don't tell anyone
m'life my life

swoop fly down
criminal waste big waste
feller fellow, person

going to the Statue of Liberty?

Alf: Me? Well, I tell ya. I always wanted to take an ocean voyage. This is a pretty big boat—bigger than the ferries—so on Sundays, sometimes, I take the trip. It's better than nothing.

Grandfather Monaghan: Thank you. [*To the kid*] So much for the great meaning of the statue, me boy. We'll talk to this lady standing at the rail. I just want you to understand why I didn't give Sheean me dime. Madam, would you be good enough to . . . Oh pardon me. [*To kid*] Better pass her by, she don't look so good. We'll ask that girl there. Young lady, if you'll pardon the curiosity of an old man . . . could you tell me in a few good words what it is about that statue that brings you out here?

Girl: What statue?

Grandfather Monaghan: Why, the Statue of Liberty up 'head. We're coming up to it.

Girl: Statue of Liberty! Is this the Statue of Liberty boat?

Grandfather Monaghan: Well, what'd you think it was?

Girl: Oh, my! I'm supposed to be on the Staten Island ferry! Where's the ticket man? [*Going away*] Ticket man! Where's the ticket man?

Child Monaghan: Gee whiz, nobody seems to want to see the statue.

Grandfather Monaghan: Just to prove it, let's see this fellow sitting on this bench here. Young man, say . . .

Young Man: I can tell you in one word. For four days I haven't had a minute's peace. My kids are screaming, my wife is yelling, upstairs they play the piano all day long. The only place I can find that's quiet is a statue. That statue is my sweetheart. Every Sunday I beat it out to the island and sit next to her, and she don't talk.

Child Monaghan: I guess you were right, grampa. Nobody seems to think it means anything.

Grandfather Monaghan: Not only doesn't mean anything, but if they'd used the money to build an honest roomin' house on that island, the immigrants would have a place to spend the night, their valises wouldn't get robbed, and they—

Megaphone Voice: Please keep your seats while the boat is docking. Statue of Liberty—all out in five minutes!

Child Monaghan: Look down there, gramp! There's a peanut stand! Could I have some?

Grandfather Monaghan:. I feel the wind comin' up. I don't think we dare

---

me boy my boy
me dime my dime

valises suitcases

Aerial View of the Statue of Liberty by Joe Viesti, Viesti Associates

take the time.

[*Music up and down*]

Child Monaghan: Ssssseuuuuuww! Look how far you can see! Look at that ship way out in the ocean!

Grandfather Monaghan: It is quite a view. Don't let go of me hand now.

Child Monaghan: I betcha we could almost see California.

Grandfather Monaghan: It's probably that grove of trees way out over there. They do say it's beyond Jersey.

Child Monaghan: Feels funny. We're standing right inside her head. Is that what you meant . . . July IV, MCD . . . ?

Grandfather Monaghan: That's it. That tablet in her hand. Now shouldn't they have put Welcome All on it instead of that foreign language? Say! Do you feel her rockin'?

Child Monaghan: Yeah, she's moving a little bit. Listen, the wind!

[*Whistling of wind*]

Grandfather Monaghan: We better get down, come on! This way!

Child Monaghan: No, the stairs are this way! Come on!

[*Running in echo. Then quick stop*]

Grandfather Monaghan: No, I told you they're the other way! Come!

Veteran: [*Calm, quiet voice*] Don't get excited, pop. She'll stand.

Grandfather Monaghan: She's swayin' awful.

Veteran: That's all right. I been up here thirty, forty times. She gives with the wind, flexible. Enjoy the view, go on.

Grandfather Monaghan: Did you say you've been up here forty times?

Veteran: About that many.

Grandfather Monaghan: What do you find here that's so interesting?

Veteran: It calms my nerves.

Grandfather Monaghan: Ah. It seems to me it would make you more nervous than you were.

Veteran: No, not me. It kinda means something to me.

Grandfather Monaghan: Might I ask what?

Veteran: Well . . . I was in the Philippine War . . . back in '98. Left my brother back there.

Grandfather Monaghan: Oh, yes. Sorry I am to hear it. Young man, I suppose, eh?

Veteran: Yeh. We were both young. This is his birthday today.

Grandfather Monaghan: Oh, I understand.

Veteran: Yeh, this statue is about the

---

betcha bet you

kinda kind of

Philippine War a war between Spain and the United States in 1898

only stone he's got. In my mind I feel it is anyway. This statue kinda looks like what we believe. You know what I mean?

Grandfather Monaghan: Looks like what we believe . . . I . . . I never thought of it that way. I . . . I see what you mean. It does look that way. [*Angrily*] See now, boy? If Sheean had put it that way I'd a give him me dime. [*Hurt*] Now, why do you suppose he didn't tell me that? Come down now. I'm sorry, sir, we've got to get out of here.

[*Music up and down*]

[*Footsteps under*]

Hurry now, I want to get out of here. I feel terrible. I do, boy. That Sheean, that fool. Why didn't he tell me that? You'd think . . .

Child Monaghan: What does this say?

[*Footsteps halt*]

Grandfather Monaghan: Why, it's just a tablet, I suppose. I'll try it with me spectacles, just a minute. Why, it's a poem, I believe . . . "Give me your tired, your poor, your huddled masses yearning to breathe free, the wretched refuse of your teeming shore. Send these, the homeless, tempest-tost to me. I lift . . . my lamp beside . . . the golden door! "Oh, dear. [*Ready to weep*] It had Welcome All on it all the time. Why didn't Sheean tell me? I'd a given him a quarter! Boy . . . go over there and here's a nickel and buy yourself a bag of them peanuts.

Child Monaghan: [*Astonished*] Gramp!

Grandfather Monaghan: Go on now, I want to study this a minute. And be sure the man gives you full count.

Child Monaghan: I'll be right back.

[*Footsteps running away*]

Grandfather Monaghan: [*To himself*] "Give me your tired, your poor, your huddled masses . . ."

[*Music swells from a sneak to full, then under to background*]

Young Monaghan. [*Soldier*] I ran over and got my peanuts and stood there cracking them open, looking around. And I happened to glance over to grampa. He had his nose right up to that bronze tablet, reading it. And

---

spectacles eyeglasses

yearning wanting, longing
wretched miserable, very poor
teeming full, crowded, busy
I'd a I'd [I would] have
them peanuts those peanuts
glance look quickly

then he reached into his pocket and kinda spied around over his eyeglasses to see if anybody was looking, and then he took out a coin and stuck it in a crack of cement over the tablet.
[*Coin falling onto concrete*]
It fell out and before he could pick it up I got a look at it. It was a half a buck. He picked it up and pressed it into the crack so it stuck. And then he came over to me and we went home.
[*Music: Change to stronger, more forceful theme*]
That's why, when I look at her now through this window, I remember that time and that poem, and she really seems to say, Whoever you are, wherever you come from, Welcome All. Welcome Home.
[*Music: Flare up to finish*]

---

spied around looked around secretively

ABOUT THE AUTHOR

Arthur Miller, who grew up in New York City, writes about important social issues—materialism (concern for money), the struggle for dignity and pride, and human rights—through his plays about family conflicts. His best-known plays include *All My Sons, The Crucible,* and *Death of a Salesman,* for which he won a Pulitzer Prize.

▶ **Arthur Miller (born 1915)** ◀

▶ *What Do You Think?*

Think about the play and discuss your ideas with your classmates and teacher. Here are some questions to talk about.

1. How would you describe the grandfather?
2. How do you know that the grandfather has a hard time admitting he's wrong?
3. How does Child Monaghan feel about his grandfather?
4. What moment in the play do you think has the most tension?
5. How does the grandfather change in the play?

▶ *Try This*

Present the story as a radio play complete with sound effects. Rehearse the play with several different people taking the parts. Note where the sound effects are, and collect items to produce the sounds of the rocking chair, boat whistle, background music, and so on.

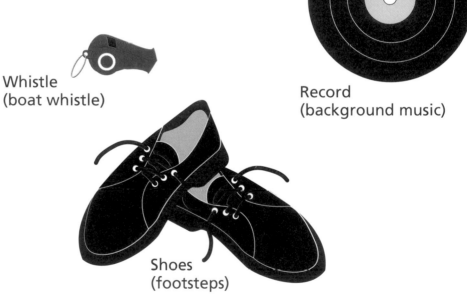

Whistle
(boat whistle)

Record
(background music)

Shoes
(footsteps)

▶ Learning About Literature

Flashbacks

A flashback occurs when past events are put into a story that takes place in the present. The events in this play are not written in the order in which they happened. The following quotations are listed in the order that they appear in the play. Which happen in the present? Which are flashbacks to an earlier time?

"We'll take the early boat, then." (p. 184)

"I ran over and got my peanuts . . ." (p. 188)

". . . he took out a coin and stuck it in a crack of cement over the tablet." (p. 189)

". . . when I look at her now through this window, I remember that time . . ." (p. 189)

▶ Writing

A Memoir with a Flashback

Use a personal memoir (perhaps your notes on an important event or your thoughts about the Statue of Liberty) to develop a memoir with a flashback.

1. Begin with a paragraph in the present in which you remember a past event.
2. Write about the past event.
3. Then write another paragraph in which you reflect on what the past event means to you.

▶ *Exploring Your Own Experience*

Walking Gallery

Draw a picture of an experience you had in which a stranger helped you. Add a caption under the picture. Then post your picture in the classroom, and discuss it with other students.

▶ *Background*

Langston Hughes once said that people of every race and in every country are generally good. In the next story, a woman helps a boy after he tries to steal from her.

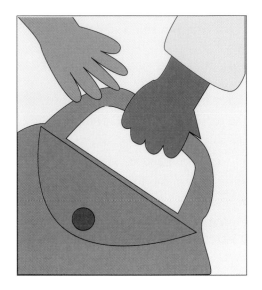

Thank You M'am

by
Langston Hughes

SHE WAS A LARGE WOMAN WITH A large purse that had everything in it but hammer and nails. It had a long strap and she carried it slung across her shoulder. It was about eleven o'clock at night, and she was walking alone, when a boy ran up behind her and tried to snatch her purse. The strap broke with the single tug the boy gave it from behind. But the boy's weight and the weight of the purse combined caused him to lose his balance so, instead of taking off full blast as he had hoped, the boy fell on his back on the sidewalk, and his legs flew up. The large woman simply turned around and kicked him right square in his blue-jeaned sitter. Then she reached down, picked the boy up by his shirt front, and shook him until his teeth rattled.

After that the woman said, "Pick up my pocketbook, boy, and give it here."

She still held him. But she bent down enough to permit him to stoop and pick up her purse. Then she said, "Now ain't you ashamed of yourself?"

Firmly gripped by his shirt front, the boy said, "Yes'm."

The woman said, "What did you want to do it for?"

The boy said, "I didn't aim to."

She said, "You a lie!"

By that time two or three people

---

slung thrown
snatch take, steal
tug pull
full blast at full speed

aim mean, plan, intend
You a lie! You're a liar!

Wilmington Evening by Aaron Bohrod, 1942

passed, stopped, turned to look, and some stood watching.

"If I turn you loose, will you run?" asked the woman.

"Yes'm," said the boy.

"Then I won't turn you loose," said the woman. She did not release him.

"I'm very sorry, lady, I'm sorry," whispered the boy.

"Um-hum! And your face is dirty. I got a great mind to wash your face for you. Ain't you got nobody home to tell you to wash your face?"

"No'm," said the boy.

"Then it will get washed this evening," said the large woman starting up the street, dragging the frightened boy behind her.

He looked as if he were fourteen or fifteen, frail and willow-wild, in tennis shoes and blue jeans.

The woman said, "You ought to be my son. I would teach you right from wrong. Least I can do right now is to wash your face. Are you hungry?"

"No'm," said the being-dragged boy. "I just want you to turn me loose."

"Was I bothering *you* when I turned that corner?" asked the woman.

"No'm."

"But you put yourself in contact with *me*," said the woman. "If you think that that contact is not going to last awhile, you got another thought coming. When I get through with you, sir, you are going to remember Mrs. Luella Bates Washington Jones."

Sweat popped out on the boy's face and he began to struggle. Mrs. Jones stopped, jerked him around in front of her, put a half nelson about his neck, and continued to drag him up the street. When she got to her door, she dragged the boy inside, down a hall, and into a large kitchenette-furnished room at the rear of the house. She switched on the light and left the door open. The boy could hear the other roomers laughing and talking in the large house. Some of their doors were open, too, so he knew he and the woman were not alone. The woman

---

I got a great mind to I'd like very much to
frail thin, weak

half nelson a wrestling hold in which one arm is placed under the opponent's arm from behind with the hand pressed against the back of the neck

still had him by the neck in the middle of her room.

She said, "What is your name?"

"Roger," answered the boy.

"Then, Roger, you go to that sink and wash your face," said the woman, whereupon she turned him loose—at last. Roger looked at the door—looked at the woman—looked at the door—*and went to the sink.*

"Let the water run until it gets warm," she said. "Here's a clean towel."

"You gonna take me to jail?" asked the boy, bending over the sink.

"Not with that face, I would not take you nowhere," said the woman, "Here I am trying to get home to cook me a bite to eat and you snatch my pocketbook! Maybe you ain't been to your supper either, late as it be. Have you?"

"There's nobody home at my house," said the boy.

"Then we'll eat," said the woman. "I believe you're hungry—or been hungry—to try to snatch my pocketbook."

"I wanted a pair of blue suede shoes," said the boy.

"Well, you didn't have to snatch *my* pocketbook to get some suede shoes," said Mrs. Luella Bates Washington Jones. "You could of asked me."

"M'am?"

The water dripping from his face, the boy looked at her. There was a long pause. A very long pause. After he had dried his face and not knowing what else to do dried it again, the boy turned around, wondering what next. The door was open. He could make a dash for it down the hall. He could run, run, run, run, *run!*

THE WOMAN WAS SITTING ON THE daybed. After a while she said, "I were young once and I wanted things I could not get."

There was another long pause. The boy's mouth opened. Then he frowned, but not knowing he frowned.

The woman said, "Um-hum! You thought I was going to say *but* didn't you? You thought I was going to say *but I didn't snatch people's pocketbooks.*

---

suede soft, fuzzy leather
You could of asked You could have asked
I were I was

Domestic Classic by Romare Bearden, 1969

Well, I wasn't going to say that." Pause. Silence. "I have done things, too, which I would not tell you, son—neither tell God, if He didn't already know. So you set down while I fix us something to eat. You might run that comb through your hair so you will look presentable."

In another corner of the room behind a screen was a gas plate and an icebox. Mrs. Jones got up and went behind the screen. The woman did not watch the boy to see if he was going to run now, nor did she watch her purse which she left behind her on the daybed. But the boy took care to sit on the far side of the room where he thought she could easily see him out of the corner of her eye, if she wanted to. He did not trust the woman *not* to trust him. And he did not want to be mistrusted now.

"Do you need somebody to go to the store," asked the boy, "maybe to get some milk or something?"

"Don't believe I do," said the woman, "unless you just want sweet milk yourself. I was going to make cocoa out of this canned milk I got here."

"That will be fine," said the boy.

She heated some lima beans and ham she had in the icebox, made the cocoa, and set the table. The woman did not ask the boy anything about where he lived, or his folks, or anything else that would embarrass him. Instead, as they ate, she told him about her job in a hotel beauty shop that stayed open late, what the work was like, and how all kinds of women came in and out, blondes, red-heads, and Spanish. Then she cut him a half of her ten-cent cake.

"Eat some more, son," she said.

WHEN THEY WERE FINISHED EATING she got up and said, "Now, here, take this ten dollars and buy yourself some blue suede shoes. And next time, do not make the mistake of latching onto my pocketbook nor nobody else's—because shoes come by devilish like that will burn your feet. I got to get my rest now. But I wish you would be-

---

set down sit down
presentable okay, satisfactory, respectable
gas plate burner for cooking
icebox early refrigerator

embarrass shame, humiliate
latching onto grabbing, holding on to
come by devilish gotten in a wicked or evil way

have yourself, son, from here on in."

She led him down the hall to the front door and opened it. "Good-night! Behave yourself, boy!" she said, looking out into the street.

The boy wanted to say something else other than, "Thank you, m'am," to Mrs. Luella Bates Washington Jones, but he couldn't do so as he turned at the barren stoop and looked back at the large woman in the door. He barely managed to say, "Thank you," before she shut the door. And he never saw her again.

stoop front steps of a house or apartment building

▶ *What Do You Think?*

Think about the story and discuss your ideas with your teacher and classmates. Below are some questions to talk about.

1. What words make Mrs. Jones seem big and powerful?

2. Is there a contrast between that power and Mrs. Jones's living situation?

3. What do you think that Roger is thinking at the beginning, middle, and end of the story? Find quotes from the story to support your ideas.

4. Can you find examples in which the author shows, but doesn't tell about the characters?

5. Do the characters in the story remind you of anyone?

6. What surprises you in the story? Is this the way you expect people to act?

7. *Dramatic tension* is created by conflict between characters and by suspense about what will happen. This tension makes you want to keep reading a good story. When do you feel tension in this story?

▶ *Learning About Literature*

A Plot Map

A plot map shows the main parts of a narrative, or story. You explored these parts in the plot profiles you made in Unit 4 (p. 143). Parts of a narrative include:

Exposition: setting, characters, and situation are revealed

Rising action: events create increasing tension

Climax: the most exciting moment

Falling action: events that work toward the ending

On the facing page is a plot map of a story you have read. With your classmates, make a plot map like the one on the facing page for "Thank You M'am." What parts of the story create dramatic tension?

Make a Plot Map

1. List the main events of the story that go with your picture of a stranger helping you, or from another story you choose.
2. Mark the places where there is tension. Usually the greatest tension is right before the climax, or most exciting moment of the story.
3. Make a plot map for your story. Briefly describe the exposition, rising action, climax, and falling action. Then add some details under each of these headings.

A Short Short Story

Use your plot map as the basis for a short short story. Try to show conflict between characters and tension about what will happen. Try to use details that show things about the characters and the setting.

A Plot Map of "The Earth on Turtle's Back"

Exposition	There was no Earth, only water. In Skyland there was a Great Tree, the Ancient Chief, and Sky Woman.
Rising Action	Sky Woman had a dream. This dream led to her falling from the sky.
Climax	The animals tried to get Earth for her. Muskrat finally succeeded.
Falling Action	The Earth placed on Turtle's back is the beginning of life on Earth.

Unit Follow-Up

▶ Making Connections

Unit Project Ideas

Here are some possible unit projects. If you want, think up a project of your own. You can use some of the techniques you learned in this unit (then and now, show don't tell, memoirs, Venn diagram, flashbacks, walking gallery, and plot map) to help you plan and complete your project.

1. Record a Radio Play. Rehearse and record *Grandpa and the Statue,* another published play, a dramatic adaptation of a story (such as "Thank You M'am"), or an original play.

2. Publish a Memoir or Character Sketch. Revise and edit an entry from your journal for publication in a magazine or for yourself.

3. Twin Memoirs. Write a memoir in two genres; for example, as a prose piece and a poem, or as a poem and a short play.

4. Graphic Art. Working with a partner, use computer graphics, collage, or your original artwork to create visual art from a cluster map or plot map. Write a caption for the work.

5. Prose into Poetry by Computer. Enter a piece of your own prose or a favorite prose selection onto the computer. Use the ENTER or RE- TURN key to experiment with different line breaks until you turn the piece into a poem you like.

6. Grandparent Stories. Working with a partner or small group, make appointments to interview staff members at school—the principal, the librarian, the custodian, and so on. Ask each person to tell a story about a grandparent or a story a grandparent used to tell. Take notes or tape record the interview. Each group member can choose a story to write down. Publish a small book of grandparent stories.

Further Reading

Here are some books related to this unit that you might enjoy.

• *A Gathering of Days: A New England Girl's Journal 1830–32,* by Joan W. Blos. Macmillan, 1979. The journal of a fourteen-year-old girl on a family farm records daily events in her small New Hampshire town, including her father's remarriage and the death of her best friend.

• *The House on Mango Street,* by Sandra Cisneros. Vintage, 1991. This collection of short stories depicts the experience of growing up as a Mexican American.

- *Now One Foot, Now the Other,* by Tomie DePaola. Putnam, 1981. A simple picture book for all ages about how a child and his grandfather help each other.

- *Homesick: My Own Story,* by Jean Fritz. Putnam, 1982. The author gives a fictionalized account, based on real events, of childhood events in China in the 1920s and 1930s that lead to her move to the United States.

- *Buffalo Woman,* by Paul Goble. Bradbury, 1984. This beautifully illustrated legend about a buffalo that turns into a beautiful woman, comes to us from the Plains Indians. It tells of the strength of family ties across cultural differences and of the kinship between humans and animals.

- *Selected Poems of Langston Hughes,* Hughes. Random House, 1959, 1990. The poems in this collection, chosen by Hughes himself shortly before his death, represent his entire career.

- *The River That Gave Gifts,* by Margo Humphrey. Children's Book Press, 1987. A group of children create presents for a respected elder. In the process they discover something about their own gifts.

- *Death of a Salesman,* by Arthur Miller. [video recording]. Castle Hill Productions, 1985. This production of Miller's Pulitzer Prize-winning play, starring Dustin Hoffman, was originally shown on television in 1986.

- *Arthur Miller Reads from* Death of a Salesman *and* The Crucible, by Arthur Miller. [audio recording]. Spoken Arts, 1968. After a brief discussion of the techniques he uses to define characters, Miller reads portions of two of his plays.

- *Hijo del Pueblo: New Mexico Poems,* by Leroy Quintana. Puerto Del Sol Press, 1976. Poems include impressions of small-town New Mexico life and the impact of modern society on the American Indian.

- *Grandfather's Stories,* by Donna Roland. Open My World Publishing, 1984–1991. The ten books in this series contain stories from Cambodia, Germany, Mexico, the Philippines, and Vietnam.

- Selected works in *The New Oxford Book of American Verse,* by William Carlos Williams. Richard Ellmann, Ed. Oxford University Press, 1976, pages 464–494. Includes "The Red Wheelbarrow" and "This Is Just to Say."

GLOSSARY

Many of the words in this Glossary have several meanings. The definitions we have used are the ones in the context in which the word appears in the book.

A

absurd foolish, silly
abuelito grandfather
according to by
aim mean, plan, intend
ain' ain't, isn't
alternating changing from one to the other
ambassador an important person sent by one country to another
ambrosia dessert made with oranges and coconut
ancient very old
anon later
anonymous unknown
apparently in a way easy to see
are y'on? Okay? Do you agree?
arrived got to
as well also, too
astonished very surprised
at large free; not caught by the police
attitudes ways of acting or feeling
awoke woke up, awakened
azaleas flowering shrubs that bloom in the spring in the South

B

barren empty
barrin' unless there is
bazaar a market or street of shops or stalls
be self-evident speak for themselves; obvious, easily understood
before I'm cold before my body gets cold when I die
benevolence kindness
betcha bet you
blessing prayer of good wishes
blind unable to see
brainstorming also called "word shaking"; listing all the words that describe a thing or feeling, used to gather many ideas in a short time
bravely not afraid
break the surface come up from under the water
brilliant shining bright
budge move

C

calligraphy beautiful handwriting
captured took prisoner
cast away thrown away
caveman, cavewoman people who lived in caves before written history
chan Japanese word that is used with names to show familiarity or fondness, like Pep*ito* in Spanish or Mik*ey* in English
chant rhythmic, repeated group of words
chants poems with rhythm and repetition that people sing or say
character each person in a story
chariots two-wheeled carts pulled by horses and used long ago for war, racing, and parades
chauffeur driver
chips potato chips or corn chips
chisel a sharp-edged tool pounded with a hammer to cut or shape wood, stone, or metal
chisel and saw tools for working with wood
chopsticks two small sticks used for eating in some Asian countries
choral reading when two or more people read a poem, a story, or a play out loud
chorus also called "refrain"; a part of a song or poem that is repeated after each stanza or verse
clustering an activity to help in writing; main idea is put at center of cluster and other ideas are added around it
come by devilish gotten in a wicked or evil way
commanded respect made people do what she wanted
composition what something is made of
concocted made up
condensed turned from gas or liquid to solid, becoming smaller and heavier
Congo country in central Africa, now called Zaire
costly expensive
creed belief
criminal waste big waste
crumples wrinkles into a ball
crust and sugar over form a hard sugar surface
curiosity need to know
custom way of acting

D

dainty small
darlin' darling, dear person, sweetheart
deferred put aside until later, postponed
departure leaving
despair deep sadness, loss of hope
disc a round, flat shape, like a plate or a wheel
disheveled messy
doan' do not
done say a mouthful said something true and
    important
dope out figure out
doubly two times; two ways
down and out feeling bad; without money or a job
drama a story written for people to act out before an
    audience
drawn pulled
ducked for cover got down behind something
dwarfed was taller than

E

eastward toward the east
ebony hard, black wood
embarrass shame, humiliate
embarrassed ashamed
embarrassing causing one to feel unhappy, self-
    conscious, or uncomfortable
emerge come out
emotion feeling
emperor ruler, king
escapade wild adventure
esta muerto he is dead
establish make, set up, start
evade escape, get away from
evaporated changed from solid or liquid to gas,
    as water when it boils
evocative bringing out a mental picture
exalted heightened, raised
eyebrows hairs directly above the eyes
eyelashes tiny hairs on an eyelid

F

faith belief
fantasy a story that could not happen in real life
feller fellow, person

fester become infected
fiery like fire
figured out discovered, found out
flashback when past events are put into a story that
    takes place in the present
fled ran away
flicked moved quickly
flinched jumped back
folktale story that teaches the right way to behave
foreign from another country
foreigner someone from another country
fragments pieces
frail thin, weak
fulfilled caused to be or happen, granted, come true
full blast at full speed
furious very angry

G

gas plate burner for cooking
genre a kind of literature
gesture movement
get attention make to look at or listen
give her a shot give her medicine with a needle
glance look quickly
gleaming shining
glittering shining
gnawed chewed
good luck charm object to bring good fortune
grasping holding
grave place where a dead person is buried
gravity the pull of the Earth which makes things fall
    back to Earth
greet to meet, welcome
gurgling water water making noise as it goes over
    rocks

H

half nelson a wrestling hold in which one arm is placed
    under the opponent's arm from behind with the hand
    pressed against the back of the neck
hamlet very small village or town
harbors has; holds
having a fit very upset
headstone marker on someone's grave
hero, heroine a person who has done something
    important to help others

GLOSSARY

hew carve, cut
hold your position stay where you are
hollow empty inside
holly leaves used to make wreaths
honored respected
hopped jumped, ran like a rabbit
howard cosell well-known U.S. TV sports announcer of
    the 1960s and 1970s
hut small house, shack

I

I got a great mind to I'd like very much to
I were I was
I'd a I would have
icebox early refrigerator
ill will bad feelings
imagery a description of something in a way that is so
    real that you can see, hear, smell, feel, or taste it
    in your mind
imagined pictured in her mind
in consequence as the effect of some cause
individual single, one at a time
inflation rising prices; when the same amount of
    money buys less than in the past
intelligent smart
interpretation your own ideas and thoughts about
    something

J

jigsaw puzzle in which all the parts fit together to make
    a whole
journal place to write down thoughts

K

kinda kind of

L

laboriously with lots of work
lame having a hurt leg or foot
latching on grabbing, holding on to
leap jump
leaping jumping
legwork going to people to get firsthand information
line of fire the line between the gun and the target;
    the path of the bullet

lived from hand to mouth (idiom) were very poor;
    only had enough food for one meal at a time
liver organ inside the body near the stomach
loaded full of
lonely feeling alone
lookin' after looking after; taking care of
lopsided crooked, bent over
lose face lose respect, feel small

M

m'life my life
magic unexplained power
make offerings give things
make up her mind decide
mansion large home of a very rich person
marbles a game with small glass balls
me boy my boy
me dime my dime
melting turning from ice into water
memoir a personal memory
meself myself
metaphor a comparison of one thing to another
meteorite rock from space
mingle mix together
mischief naughty fun
molehill small pile of dirt
monotonous boring; the same thing over and over
    again
mum's the word don't tell anyone
mysterious unexplained, strange
myths stories that people tell to explain why things are
    the way they are

N

narrative writing that tells a story
nebulae more than one nebula
neglected left out, not done
Nome No, ma'am
nonfiction writing writing about true events

O

obediently following the rules
observe follow, act by
obviously in a way easy to see
occurred happened, came to be

omen sign

orbiting circling or moving around something

origami Japanese art of paper folding

outstretched extended, opened, reaching

overjoyed very happy

P

P.S. Public School

pale softly colored

paradise heaven

parasols umbrellas used as shades

pause wait for a moment when reading

pedestal support

perpetual care when people pay cemetery owners to take care of graves forever

perplexed confused, not understanding

pestering bothering

pharaohs rulers in Egypt long ago

Philippine War a war between Spain and the United States in 1898

piñones pine nuts

playwright the author of a play

plot what happens in a story

point of view understanding of the situation

possession something one owns

power strength

precious costly, dear, expensive

prepared got ready

presentable okay, satisfactory, respectable

previous earlier, one before

prodigious wonderful, amazing, very large

proof test of the truth; facts that show the truth

prose speech or writing that does not have rhyme or meter and is not poetry

pursuers chasers

put it say it

putting in giving money

Q

quickwrite writing thoughts as they come without stopping

quizzical questioning

R

radiation sickness illness caused by dangerous particles from atomic weapons

rallies when many people get together to show support for an idea

rank bad-smelling

raw uncooked

Readers' Theater one person reads a story while other people act out the roles and read the characters' words

records phonograph albums or recordings of music or instruction

refrain also called "chorus"; a part of a song or poem that is repeated after each stanza or verse

reputation way people think about you

rewarded gave a nice surprise to

ridiculous very laughable

ring sound, fill the air

rioting when many people are in a fight, often with property damaged and people hurt

ripped it open tore it open

risk chance

rites important ceremonies usually done the same way each time, such as wedding or funeral rites

rotating spinning, turning around

rough difficult

rousing waking up

ruby red precious stone

run me out given me a ride

S

sacred holy

sags hangs down

Santa Claus Father Christmas; bearded man in red suit said to bring Christmas gifts

schoolmistress female school principal

scolded criticized, spoke angrily

scorned rejected, looked down on, purposely ignored

scurried ran away

segregation laws laws that kept blacks and whites apart

set down sit down

shamed lose respect, feel small

shed tears cried

shivering shaking from the cold

sho' do it sure does

simile a comparison using the word *like* or *as*

slung thrown

snatch take, steal

snuck went very quietly so no one would see

snuff a form of smokeless tobacco

sore wound; injury; hurt place

spectacles eyeglasses

spied around looked around secretly

spotted saw

spreading enlarging or expanding to cover more space

stanza a group of lines in a poem used to separate ideas

stay clear of avoid, stay away from

stingiest most unwilling to spend money, cheapest

stoop front steps of a house or apartment building

story map a chart or picture showing the main elements in a story

streak long, thin strip

strengths good parts

stretched out reached out

stretched reached out

subdivision a small planned neighborhood in which the houses were built at about the same time

suede soft, fuzzy leather

suffered withstood but not easily

supersonic faster than sound

sway move from side to side

swindle trick to get someone's money

swirling going around and around

swoop fly down

symbol a picture or word that stands for something else

system group in a pattern

T

tacks small, round candies that come on strips of paper

taken back (idiom) surprised, shocked

tame make something wild into something domesticated, as one tames an animal to be a pet

teeming full, crowded, busy

Temple Sisterhood service club run by Jewish women

temples places to worship God

the Garden Club neighborhood organization for women

the Junior League service organization for women

the sacred directions the holy directions: north, south, east, and west

them peanuts those peanuts

theme a writer's message

theories best guesses based on scientific study

theory a scientist's guess based on facts and observations

thereafter after that

they their

third person limited point of view the teller is not in the story, yet tells facts that only the characters would know

through in one side and out the other side of

tilted slanted

tin foil aluminum foil or wrap

tiniest very smallest

to be over with to end, to be finished

tomb grave, burial place

tough hard to chew

treachery trickery

trembling shaking

trifle a small or unimportant thing or item

trowel garden tool for digging

tug pull

tumbled tossed and churned

twinkling shining, sparkling

U

undoubtedly without a doubt, definitely true

uniform special clothes for school or work

unique like no other

unveiled uncovered, shown

uprooted taken out of the ground

V

valises suitcases

varicolored many-colored

various different

Venn diagram uses circles to show similarities and differences between topics

virtually nearly, almost completely

W

wade walk in shallow water

weary tired

weeping cherry cherry tree with long branches that hang down like tears

widow a woman whose husband has died

word shaking also called "brainstorming"; listing all the words that describe a thing or feeling, used to gather many ideas in a short time

worthily in a good way

wreath circle of leaves or branches people put on their doors and windows at Christmas time

wretched miserable, very poor

Y

yapping talking (like a noisy little dog)

yearning wanting, longing

You a lie! You are a liar!

You could of asked You could have asked

ACKNOWLEDGMENTS

Text

Unit 1

5 *The Way to Start a Day* by Byrd Baylor. Reprinted with permission of Charles Scribner's Sons, an imprint of Macmillan Publishing company from *The Way To Start a Day* by Byrd Baylor. Text copyright ©1977, 1976 Byrd Baylor. (Text appeared in McCall's Magazine, Feb. 1977)

17 "Here Comes the Sun" by George Harrison. Copyright © 1969 HARRISONGS LTD. International Copyright Secured. All rights reserved.

23 "Prospective Immigrants, Please Note" is reprinted from *Snapshots of a Daughter-in-Law, Poems 1954–1962*, by Adrienne Rich, by permission of W.W. Norton & Company, Inc. Copyright ©1956, 1957, 1958, 1959, 1960, 1961, 1962, 1963, 1967 by Adrienne Rich Conrad.

29 "China's Little Ambassador" from *In the Year of the Boar and Jackie Robinson* by Bette Bao Lord. Text copyright © 1984 by Bette Bao Lord. Illustrations Copyright © by Marc Simont. Reprinted by permission of HarperCollins Publishers.

Unit 2

43 "There Are No People Song" reprinted from *The Sky Clears* by A. Grove Day, by permission of University of Nebraska Press. Copyright ©1951 by A. Grove Day.

49 "The Earth on Turtle's Back" from *Keepers of the Earth: Native American Stories and Environmental Activities for Children* by Michael J. Caduto and Joseph Bruchac. Fulcrum Publishing, 350 Indiana Street, #350 Golden CO 80401.

58–64 "The Fire Stealer," "Pan Ku," and "Prometheus" retold by Pat Rigg reprinted by permission of Pat Rigg.

67 "How the Mayans Got Fire and Fooled Their Enemies" from *Forestville Tales* by Aaron Berman. Illustrations by Harry Rosenbaum by permission of Heinle & Heinle Publishers. Copyright ©1977 Collier MacMIllan International.

75 "Birth of the Moon" by Heather Couper and Nigel Henbest from *Space Scientist: The Moon* reprinted by permission of Franklin Watts, Ltd., U.K.

Unit 3

87 *Driving Miss Daisy* by Alfred Uhry. Reprinted by permission of Terry Nemeth, Theatre Communications Group.

97 "Oath of Friendship" from *Translations from the Chinese* by Arthur Waley. Copyright ©1919 and renewed 1947 by Arthur Waley. Reprinted by permission of Alfred A. Knopf, Inc.

99 "Bridge Over Troubled Water" by Paul Simon. Copyright ©1969 Paul Simon. Used by permission of the publisher.

105 Excerpts and illustrations from *The Little Prince* by Antoine de Saint-Exupéry, copyright ©1943 and renewed 1971 by Harcourt Brace Jovanovich, Inc., reprinted by permission of the publisher.

115 "A Brave Man Lays His Life on the Line," by S. Avery Brown and Joe Treen. Reprinted by permission of People Weekly 1991, S. Avery Brown and Joe Treen.

Unit 4

125 "Dreams" from *The Dream Keeper and Other Poems* by Langston Hughes. Copyright ©1932 by Alfred A. Knopf, Inc. and renewed 1960 by Langston Hughes. Reprinted by permission of the publisher.

127 "Dream Deferred" from *The Panther and the Lash: Poems of Our Times* by Langston Hughes. Copyright ©1951 by Langston Hughes. Reprinted by permission of Alfred A. Knopf, Inc.

133 "The Carpenter's Son" by Mohammed Reshad Wasa from *Folk Tales from Asia for Children Everywhere Book 3*. Reprinted by permission of Weatherhill, Inc.

143 "I Have a Dream" (abridged version) by Dr. Martin Luther King, Jr. Copyright ©1963 by Dr. Martin Luther King, Jr. Renewed 1991 by Coretta Scott King. Reprinted by permission of Joan Daves Agency.

149 "The Golden Crane" from *Sadako and the Thousand Paper Cranes*. Copyright ©1977 by Eleanor Coerr. Illustrations copyright © 1977 by Ronald Himler. Reprinted by permission of G.P. Putnam's Sons.

Unit 5

161 "Piñones" by Leroy Quintana. Originally published in *New Mexico Magazine.* Permission requested from author, unobtained at time of publication.

167 "The Last Words of My English Grandmother" by William Carlos Williams from *The Collected Poems of William Carlos Williams, 1909–1939, vol. I.* Copyright ©1938 by New Directions Publishing Corporation. Reprinted by permission of New Directions Publishing Corporation.

175 "Papa Who Wakes Up in the Dark" from *The House on Mango Street,* published in the U.S. by Vintage, a division of Random House, Inc., New York and distributed in Canada by Random House of Canada Limited, Toronto. Originally published in somewhat different form in ARTE PUBLICO PRESS in 1984 and revised in 1989. Reprinted with permission of Susan Bergholz, Bergholz Literary Services, New York, NY.

181 Excerpted from "Grandpa and the Statue" by Arthur Miller. Reprinted by permission of International Creative Management, Inc. Copyright ©1945 by Arthur Miller. Copyright renewed.

193 "Thank you, M'am" by Langston Hughes. Reprinted by permission of Harold Ober Associates Incorporated. Copyright ©1958 by Langston Hughes. Copyright renewed 1986 by George Houston Bass.

Art

cover Tate Gallery, London/Art Resource, NY; **2** Collection of Paul Jacques Schupf. Courtesy of the Marlborough Gallery; **6** ©1991 David Muench; **11** Art Resource, NY; **13** Courtesy of Macmillan Publishing Company; **18** ©The Phillips Collection, Washington, D.C.; **19** Globe Photos; **24** Yale University Art Gallery, Bequest of Stephen Carlton Clark; **25** Annie F. Valva/W.W. Norton & Company; **32** Courtesy of the National Museum of American Art, Washington, D.C./Art Resource, NY; **35** ©1981 Jim Kalett; **40** van Gogh, Vincent. The Starry Night. (1889) Oil on canvas, 29 x 36 1/4" (73.7 x 92.1 cm). Collection, The Museum of Modern Art, New York. Acquired through the Lillie P. Bliss Bequest; **44** © Galen Rowell/Mountain Light Photography; **50** Photo courtesy of the National Museum of American Art. From the Weeks Family Collection; **53** ©Dan Hunting/Fulcrum Publishing (t); ©Carol Bruchac/Fulcrum Publishing (b); **59** Hudson's Bay Company Archives, Provincial Archives of Manitoba. Ref.# P 181; **62** ©1991 Steven Hunt/Image Bank; **65,68** Photo by Hillel Burger. Peabody Museum, Harvard University; **76** NASA; **84** Courtesy of the artist; **88,92** Movie Still Archives; **93** Flora Roberts Photography; **98** ©1992 The Estate of Keith Haring; **100** ©Mike Mazzaschi/Stock Boston; **101** ©Jim Pozarik/Gamma-Liaison; **106,109** Illustration from *The Little Prince* by Antoine de Saint-Exupéry, copyright 1943 and renewed 1971 by Harcourt Brace Jovanovich, Inc., reproduced by permission of the publisher; **116** ©1991 Stella Johnson/PEOPLE Weekly; **117** Copyright ©1989 Esme (b); PEOPLE Weekly ©1992 (t); **122** ©1992 Succession H. Matisse/ARS, NY; **126** ©Galen Rowell/Mountain Light Photography; **128** Dallas Museum of Art, Dallas Art Association Purchase; **129** Springer/Bettmann Film Archive; **134** Hermitage, St. Petersburg/The Bridgeman Art Library; **138** Pushkin Museum, Moscow/The Bridgeman Art Library; **144** Ben Shahn. Welders. (1943). Tempera on cardboard mounted on composition board, 22 x 39 3/4", (55.9 x 100.9 cm). Collection, The Museum of Modern Art, New York. Purchase; **145** UPI/Bettmann Newsphotos; **150** Courtesy of the Phyllis Kind Gallery, Chicago; **152** ©P.J. Griffiths/Magnum Photos; **153** Courtesy of the Putnam & Grosset Group; **158** Anna Mary Robertson ("Grandma") Moses (1860–1961) Christmas at Home. Copyright ©1989, Grandma Moses Properties Co., New York. Grandma Moses became famous in old age for her paintings of rural America; **162** ©John Cancalosi/Stock Boston; **171** Photo by Charles Sheeler. Courtesy of New Directions Publishing Corporation; **176** Edward Hopper. Man Seated on Bed. c.1905–6. oil on board. 11 x 8 7/8" Collection of Whitney Museum of American Art, New York. Josephine N. Hopper Bequest; **177** Photo by Rubin Guzman; **182** Courtesy of The Brooklyn Historical Society; **186** ©Joe Viesti/Viesti Associates, Inc.; **189** ©Inge Morath/Magnum Photos; **194** Aaron Bohrod. Wilmington Evening. 1942. Courtesy of the Corcoran Gallery of Art, Washington, D.C.; **197** Courtesy of the Bearden Estate.